Praise for Th

"To work as a witch means to embrace liminality, always moving between various states and layers of reality. Touching on thirteen different areas of a witch's practice, Christine Grace's exploration of what it means to occupy a place in the natural world challenges readers to think about specific aspects of their practice in a focused way. *The Witch at the Forest's Edge* is a welcome and thought-provoking addition to a modern library, enabling a practitioner to re-examine their spiritual connection to the natural world at any point in their journey."

—Arin Murphy-Hiscock, author of *The Green Witch*

"One of my many hats is as a forest farmer, so *The Witch at the Forest's Edge* by Christine Grace has a special meaning for me. I grew up as a forest dweller and live now with the woods at my back porch. This powerful and intensely liminal place holds the keys to a deepening of our spirituality as well as a broadening of it. This book will be read, marked, pondered upon, and read again."

—H. Byron Ballard, author of *Seasons of a Magical Life*

"'We've never truly existed beyond the reach of enchantment,' says Christine Grace early in this captivating book. A genuine exploration of enchantment through the experience of modern traditional witchcraft is the gift that she offers us. *The Witch at the Forest's Edge* is accessible but deep work, and Grace does not shy away from encouraging us to be open to more demanding practices and fields of study. We are ushered from known to unknown, stepping into liminal spaces and weaving rituals that strengthen our spiritual work and relationships. Ample opportunity for reflection exists within these pages, as well, with insightful questions attributed to each 'key,' making this an excellent book for seasoned witches, alongside those just starting down the path. I am so impressed by the guidance offered here—we are escorted along the hedge by the author's lamplight of wisdom and offered myriad ways to discover the treasures of magic for ourselves. What a journey!"

—Jen Rue Holmes, of *Rue and Hyssop*

"A thoughtful examination of witchcraft, *The Witch at the Forest's Edge* by Christine Grace explores a wide range of topics from sourcing our tools ethically to examining the origins of what we *think* we know to discovering the spirits of place. Grace's gentle voice evokes a texture of dappled shade, as though these truths were shared on the border between this world and the next. *The Witch at the Forest's Edge* restores the animalia missing from pop culture witchcraft, linking nature's richness with modern understandings of community, respect for culture, and stewardship."
—Amy Blackthorn, author of Blackthorn's *Botanical Magic*

"*The Witch at the Forest's Edge* by Christine Grace presents a thorough one-on-one introduction to the Forest's Edge Tradition's approach to modern witchcraft, while wonderfully adding to the conversation surrounding the execution and usefulness of a regional, animist-based practice."
—Christopher Orapello, coauthor of *Besom, Stang, and Sword* and cohost of the *Down at the Crossroads* podcast

"The witch is a curious figure, existing in a uniquely liminal space of both fact and fiction, this world and the next. Many practitioners of magic walk a path that carefully stays in that middle ground, but a few heed the call to peek beyond the hedge, to walk amongst ancestors and spirits and gods and beings for which we don't yet have names. It can be daunting to leave that comfortable middle path, but Christine Grace's book *The Witch at the Forest's Edge* provides a gentle, encouraging hand to hold as you take your first steps past the hedge into the world beyond. The advice is practical, grounded in a practice that begins with what you have on hand and in your surroundings, includes discussion of ancestry and the many ways that family is made and found, and includes a deeply appreciated section on magical ethics. This book is practical, fresh, and will help guide a whole new generation off the well-trod path to embrace the old, wild magic found beyond the hedge."
—Fire Lyte, author of *The Dabbler's Guide to Witchcraft* and host of *Inciting A Riot*

THE
WITCH
AT THE
FOREST'S
EDGE

THE
WITCH
AT THE
FOREST'S
EDGE

Thirteen Keys to
Modern Traditional Witchcraft

CHRISTINE GRACE

Foreword by Cory Thomas Hutcheson

WEISER BOOKS

This edition first published in 2021 by Weiser Books, an imprint of
Red Wheel/Weiser, LLC
With offices at:
65 Parker Street, Suite 7
Newburyport, MA 01950
www.redwheelweiser.com

ISBN: 978-1-57863-758-4

Library of Congress Cataloging-in-Publication Data available upon request.

Cover design by Kathryn Sky-Peck
Interior by Deborah Dutton
Typeset in Adobe Garamond Pro, Apercu Pro, and Nexa Rust Sans

Printed in the United States of America
IBI
10 9 8 7 6 5 4 3 2 1

To my magical, beloved family

Contents

This book would not exist without Marijean Rue. Her spirit and wisdom suffuse the work. We wrote teaching material together for years prior to the writing of the book, and the ideas and practices herein have been shaped within our nourishing friendship and co-leadership. Cory Hutcheson's support and assistance helped me see the broader potential of this work, and Gabriel Whalen insisted on the validity of my voice even when I doubted.

I am grateful to the members of the Forest's Edge Tradition, to its spirit, and to the Voices, its guiding council. I am grateful to my apprentices for teaching me and to the ancestors for guiding me. I am grateful to the forest for enfolding me, and to my family for loving me.

Foreword

Coming to the forest is a powerful experience for me. The trees rise high above my head, spreading out their branches to form a natural cathedral. All around me I feel the woods breathing, life spilling out from between roots and under rocks, the soft sigh of fungi and bacteria reclaiming fallen logs or creatures and bringing them back home into the soil. The forest is a place of wonder. Once, when heading to a crossroads for a nighttime magical working, I stopped suddenly, deeply aware that something was watching me from the edge of the forest. My breath hitched in my chest as I saw a deer—a stag—emerge from between the trees with tall, wide antlers like a crown on his head. He stood and watched me for a moment, and then—almost like a dream—he stepped backwards into the forest and disappeared, evaporating into the dark spaces between the bark and leaves. In another instance, my magical partner and I were doing some work in a small forest near our homes, and we had gotten a bit turned around. We turned off our flashlights and paused, asking for guidance or help. When we turned the lights on again, a juvenile deer stood there a few feet in front of us, then turned and led us in the direction we needed to go. The forest is a place of deep magic. That magic can be powerful, and also frightening. It is always good to have a guide.

Christine Grace's book sits in your hands now, the product of years of working within the various forests of witchcraft. Some are quite literal, as she lives the enviable life of a woodlands-dwelling witch in her log cabin with her wild witchlets. Some are forests deeper within us that can be even trickier to navigate than the wilderness of scrub pines and pioneer poplars. She is meeting you here at the edge of the forest to guide you deeper within, show you the path that she has marked, and teach you how to make your own trails in magic. I have been lucky enough to benefit from her guidance directly, as she has been a teacher, mentor, and friend to me for several years. Within the tradition of the Forest's Edge, learning magic and witchcraft comes through the practice of apprenticeship. We take our time, valuing the slow and thorough way that witchcraft opens up to us as practitioners learning to navigate the hedge space between the worlds. We gain from one another's experience, help each other cross through the thresholds between the seen and unseen, and even occasionally sit in our kitchens sipping tea and swapping folk charms. This is witchcraft on a simmer, witchcraft that knits together stitch-by-stitch over time, witchcraft that looks up through the trees in each season to see a different moon. This book will be like that, and you will have to do the work to gain the magic, sometimes pushing yourself or shifting into the shadows to learn how deeply enchantment can root. There is risk in the way we become witches in the Forest's Edge, but there is also reward.

In fairy tales, going into the forest is often a transformative experience. Hansel and Gretel are abandoned by their parents, only to confront a wicked witch and overcome her cannibalistic plans. When they return home, an oft-forgotten element of the story involves Gretel summoning a duck to carry them both across the river, showing that her encounter with the witch may have left her with a few new skills of her own. Similarly, in the Slavic tales of Baba Yaga and Vasilissa, the young woman apprentices with the ancient witch, doing work for and with her, until finally she is freed to return home with a magical fire that incinerates her wicked stepsisters plus the power to make cloth so fine it appears Otherworldly (and probably is). We go into the forest to change ourselves, to grow and confront our fears.

This book is also transformative. It is not meant to be something you simply read, but a text that prompts action, encounter, and change. Christine Grace offers you lessons to understand the land around you (whether it has actual forest or not); learn to listen to intuition and use divination to expand your knowledge, craft spells and rituals that will hold deep meaning for you; and follow in the tradition of hedge-crossing witches of the past, present, and (hopefully) future. Each section will also ask you to respond to questions with thought and effort and to do specific work to put these lessons to use in your life. This is magic rooted in experience, in folklore, in history, in tradition, and—crucially—in change. What Grace gives you is more than just a path to follow; it is a full set of tools to mark your own trail past the Forest's Edge and into the wilderness of witchcraft. You will know the power of wild and holy places by the time you finish this book and may even find some powerful magic growing in your home or just beyond your back door.

This book can offer you much, but will only take you part of the way. It asks you to do the work of witching, while keeping your feet steady as you cross the threshold into new and wildly enchanted landscapes. It is a beautiful book, and maybe even a slightly terrifying one (in the best possible way). I am so excited for you to read it and so thankful you have Grace with you here as you cross into the deep, dark woods.

Welcome to the Forest's Edge. Blessings to you upon your way.

—Cory Thomas Hutcheson, author of *New World Witchery*

Introduction

I stand in the meadow, at the forest's edge. One step forward and I will straddle the boundary between fading light in the swaying grass and rich darkness in the woods. One more step and I will be immersed in the nighttime world of southern, hardwood forest. My home lies behind me, the wild magic ahead. I am the witch at the Forest's Edge.

It could be that you are also a witch at the forest's edge. A witch at the forest's edge weaves magic from the between-places. We are most at home between the realities of daily life and ecstasies of enchantment. Between deadlines and drumbeats, hearthstones and electric stoves, front steps and the forest deep. We are everywhere and nowhere. We are ancient and modern. We are domestic and wild. We are crooked, cock-eyed, and quirky. We are rooted. We are powerful.

Many witches seek a path of deep, transformative magic and a way to be fiercely independent, together. Modern traditional witchcraft is a broad term that speaks to the particularity of each witch:

your own ecosystem of location, ancestry, identity, and influence. It speaks of spirit-led witches who see enchantment everywhere. It calls to those who are rooted in folklore and bioregion and those who draw on the deep past to weave a modern path. This is my way and the way of my tradition. It is what I have set out in this book as a framework for your own unique path.

My route into this way of working has been winding, but over time my practice has grown, the magical community has grown, and the access we all have to information has blossomed into something previously unimaginable. The opportunities are wonderful, but the breadth and variety can become overwhelming. The aesthetics can compete with the practicalities, and as life carries on and responsibilities increase, many of us find our practices can fade for a season. Consider this book a skeletal framework to organize and ground your explorations in our busy times. The plethora of books, archives, articles, podcasts, videos, and social media feeds are tools to add flesh to the bones I've set out here. These chapters contain what I treat as the foundational ideas of my kind of modern, traditional witchcraft. I didn't set out to write a book, or stare at a screen willing the ideas to come. Instead, the book has grown from decades of real practice and teaching. I wrote it down, simply because it works.

This is a demanding book and a demanding path. I often send readers to do their own research and experimentation on sundry topics of interest, but such is a way of witchery that honors the authentic ties of each individual to region and ancestry. It is easier to be told and harder to do. But we all know witchcraft is work—powerful, satisfying work.

The Forest's Edge Tradition

The ideas in this book are an invitation to all the animists, ancestor worshipers, magic seekers, and wild at heart. They are also foundational to a small, initiatory tradition of witchcraft called The Forest's Edge, that I co-founded in 2011. We emerged from the leadership of an earlier tradition and founded our new venture on ideals of inclusive, broad leadership within a green, animist, shamanic, and traditional path. We strive for deep, transformative practice combined with thoughtful mediation of group dynamics. The Forest's Edge tradition is guided by a council and two co-leaders, of which I am one. Our initiates share an individualized method of teaching and a relationship with an *egregore*, the living spirit of the tradition.

Many witches find their way to us because they hunger for a thorough and accessible approach to traditional witchcraft with teachers who are experienced but not dogmatic. Unfotunately, the interest from the broader community outstrips our initiates' availability to teach and mentor. This book aims to meet that need in new way. The tradition is not the book and vice versa but know that the contents of this book have been tested time and again through the work of the tradition.

The essence of the Forest's Edge way is to honor the specificity of the individual, while holding that each witch is fully themselves only within the web of human and Other relationships in which we live and have our being. Our way of witchcraft is not inherently religious, although all are encouraged to reflect on their relationship with the idea of gods. Some draw on the traditions of recent ancestors, such as Christian folk magic; some reach back to the gods of the ancients; and still others remain agnostic. We are all united by the understanding that everything has a spirit, and the world is infused with magic.

How to Use This Book

As a teacher, I work hard to teach in a way that allows both novice and experienced witches to refine and deepen their personal practices. This book strives to do the same. An experienced witch may skip many exercises or may be able to imagine their own, but I encourage experienced witches to find their growing edges and lean into them. A growing edge is the threshold between what is familiar and what is new. Identify something that feels challenging, interesting, or novel and go deep. Read widely, reflect, and practice. If you disagree with me, consider writing me a letter as a journaling exercise to refine and sharpen your position, or discuss it with a witch you know. One of the glories of teaching, apprenticing, and being part of a tradition is being able to bounce ideas around. For some solitary practitioners, journaling and online discussion may be your best means.

For the newer practitioner, know that newness does not equal inferiority or a lack of power. You are bringing your own knowledge, abilities, and background, and those are wonderful things. You and your world are already full of magic. I encourage you to skim the beginning of each chapter but recommend reading them in order. I do rearrange the order of subjects for individual apprentices, but here I have presented the material in the way that is most helpful for newcomers.

Alongside typical witchy skillsets of spellcraft, divination, and ritual observances, you will find that this book treats hedgeriding (spirit flight or shamanism) and ritual possession as essential, teachable skills. And alongside the typical witchy love of plants and gardens, you will find tools to connect to your local, wild ecosystem no matter where you live. After an overview of a witchy worldview, we'll explore spirit work and jump right into the concept of spiritual ancestry because your own sense of connection to history will guide your choices through the later chapters.

Self-Assessment

The first step toward the forest's edge is to consider where you are right now. It is much easier to choose goals for your practice and to find opportunities for growth after some self-reflection. Whether you are impressively experienced or an uncommitted explorer, the goal is not self-judgment but an accepting awareness. Just notice what is true for you right now. Think through the answers, journal, or discuss with a friend.

1. Consider your previous Craft-related study. Do you have particular areas of expertise or interest? What are the sources of your learning so far (direct experience, books, teachers, groups)? What learning experiences have or have not worked for you? Why?

2. Reflect on your current personal and communal practice. Do you practice solitary? With a group? Does one way dominate the other? Is your practice spontaneous? Scheduled? What do you love about it right now? What could be different?

3. What are your strengths as a witch?

4. What are your gaps, weaknesses, or places for growth as a witch?

5. How do you think reading this book can help you address the gaps in your praxis (the recurrent cycle of practice and reflection through which we all grow), and make the most of your strengths?

6. What are your goals for your practice of witchcraft?

7. How would you describe your learning style? Do you learn best by doing new things? By reading? Through conversation?

8. What kind of witch are you? (This question is intentionally vague. Answer it in any way that resonates with you.)

Welcome to the forest's edge. May your way be enchanted and your power extraordinary.

1

WORLDVIEW AND SPIRITUALITY

The world is enchanted, filled with the whisperings of spirits. We witches are alive in a vibrant world, and we find meaning and power in our relationships with all beings. Our form of spirituality is a living relationship with spirits—the animating, dynamic, sacred essences within all things and beyond. Wonder, mystery, and sacredness co-exist with and inhabit our perception, from the most mundane to the most extraordinary aspects of our lives. As witches of the Forest's Edge, we work unabashedly and intensely with real magic, and we are profoundly shaped by our Craft.

This chapter has a theoretical bent, while many of the others speak more directly to the day-to-day doings of witchery. The point is not to bog down practice with navel-gazing, but rather to be transparent about some of the ideas that underlie the practicalities of subsequent chapters. The themes of enchantment, interconnectedness, and liminality are currents running throughout the book. The notion of a witch's spirituality as something that we *do* is reflected in my emphasis on practicality. Throughout, you will find a dynamic balance of pragmatism and deep understanding.

Many witches are of a rational, bookish, and, quite frankly, nerdy bent. We place a high value on science, critical thought, and careful discernment. Yet also, the immediacy of our experience tells us that there is more wonder than we can describe. We possess more agency than we would ever hope, and so do other beings. And as peculiar as it may seem to folks of a different worldview, our way of being can be intensely fulfilling to us, and living fully into it can be a profound homecoming.

Enchantment

As Western culture moved toward modernity, we moved away from enchantment, or seeing the sacredness everywhere. With this movement, we have enjoyed the blossoming of science and the championing of critical thought, but for the most part we have lost a world full of charm and mystery. We could treasure science, critical thinking, and secularism, and also a worldview of connection and enchantment. But here we are in a world where wonder is called childlike and dismissed as immature. How much more could the world flourish if we let the freedom and understanding of rationality breed wonder, humility, and relationship?

The truth is that we humans have never been good at being modern even in the most Westernized regions of the world. We've never believed with our whole hearts that only humans are conscious and that the cosmos is a spiritless machine. We've never really all decided that there is no way of sensing beyond the ordinary senses and that we've never truly existed beyond the reach of enchantment. Right now, people are talking to their cats, feeling that a certain tree is a particularly good place beneath which to rest, and wearing lucky socks.

Instead of being an antidote to this problem, too much of modern religion drains wonder from the world. When religion becomes a matter of belief in disembodied religious ideas and moral purity, then it does not matter at all if a religious person lives in the world as if they appreciate the sacredness in ordinary life. But we witches shake off *religion as purity of belief.* We shake off the twisting of science into a tool for domination. We embrace the sacredness, the wonder, and the magic of everyday life. We embrace enchantment.

Interconnectedness

A peculiar thing happens when we embrace enchantment. Enchantment lends itself to seeing the real, the personal, the active, and the intentional everywhere. We start to see the ways in which we have mistakenly treated ourselves as the most real beings, the center of the world, while acting as though the rest of the world is just made of things.

This self-centering does have use in magic, to help us fully appreciate our power and connectedness, but it is a metaphor for our agency—or our ability to do things. We do this self-centering in relation to other humans and also to other-than-human parts of the cosmos and not as though it applies only to us. While it may seem like a powerful superiority, this self-centeredness is not only harmful to others but also leaves us feeling isolated and powerless. So many of us mostly interact with other humans and with the creations of humans, we develop the sickness of separation from nature. It is a painful delusion to think we are separate.

We witches of the Forest's Edge seek to find our place within the world, not on a pedestal above it. And indeed, to be fully immersed in the world is to be powerful, not because you seek to dominate, horde, and exploit, but because you are a sovereign doer among doers, working with the strength of those relationships.

It is easy to slide back into the self-centering habit of treating others as objects, tools, or mirrors of the self. As witches, we strive to engage with others as a spirit in relationship with another spirit, nature to nature, or person to person. Following from this way of seeing all beings as real, personal, and active, we draw on the ways that we are interconnected with all of these spirits. All things are interrelated, and we work with this when doing magic. This is not because of a god that connects or contains everything, but simply because the nature of nature is ecological interconnectedness.

Perhaps it is strange to use a term from science, *ecology*, to describe spirituality, but I don't think it is odd for a witch. It is an apt way to conceptualize our relationships with others. Ecology has an etymology that lends itself to a poetic understanding. *Eco-* comes from the Greek *oikos*, meaning home, or, to go back even earlier to the *Proto-Indo-European* (PIE) root, it means clan. Linguists have reconstrusted PIE as a common ancestor language to many modern languages, including English. Meanwhile, *-logy* has a richer history than just "study of." It means word or speaking. From the PIE root, it means to gather. So, with ecology, we are speaking of home, we are gathering with our clan. Allow yourself to be gathered home, nestled in with your more-than-human kin, so that the world can become enchanted before your eyes. We are most fully human when we are at home as one part of nature on earth.

Accepting your place as one piece within the natural world is glorious but not easy. It requires a sacrifice of the ideals of human society that hold us up as more than nature. And as part of nature, we are part of systems that can be dangerous and bloody. But that doesn't mean we're victims. We are doers, and witches are dangerous, too. This sense of connection and appreciation for other-than-human beings locates the witch as a self-in-community with others, but it does not deny the specificity of any person, human or otherwise.

Liminality

Witches are threshold dwellers. We are liminal, which means that we can be present on both sides of a boundry. It means we stand in a transformative space betwixt and between. That's what liminal means and what it means to be at the forest's edge.

By seeking the enchanting magic of relatedness to others while we embrace literacy, logic, science, and personal freedom, we often find ourselves at the edges of contemporary society. We are both logical and pursuing experience far beyond what could be explained by society's logic. We are also, in many ways, a tremendously normal bunch—with jobs, kids, homes, hobbies, and any number of other things that fill our lives—just like everyone else. But we can walk in both worlds and weave them together in the living of our lives. And as edge-dwellers, we stand in good company with ancestors, whose magical practices set them just a bit apart from the rest of the community, and with the ecological edges between different habitats.

Religion and Spirituality in Community

Likely it will come as little surprise that I, along with many witches, struggle with the concept of religion. If religion is primarily dogma, offering a strict list of required beliefs and crystal clear dos and do nots, then the practice of witchery set forth in this book is *not* about religion. Or if religion is primarily hierarchy, maintaining hard boundaries between those who are able to understand and connect directly with the sacred and those who must follow only the ones with superior knowledge, then this is *not* about religion.

Any conception of religion—and there are many—that creates an impenetrable barrier between this thing and that, or that draws clear, comfortable lines between those who are in or out, cannot stand within the realm of the Forest's Edge. For we witches embrace a self-definition that places us on the boundary. We seek the immediacy of direct experience. We encourage diversity of thought and practice. We emphasize the specificity of an individual's craft and hold all initiates as equals. That said, if religion is a collection of ideas, practices, ethics, texts, and organizational systems that seeks to help connect humankind with the sacred or the spiritual, then indeed our variety of witchery is much like religion.

On the subject of spirituality, in self-help or New Age publications, spirituality is often understood as your own relationship with your higher self or the cultivation of a purer, less ego-driven inner self. In contrast, we would say that individual self-improvement is a product of powerful spiritual engagement but not the end in itself. The witch's spirituality is about transformative magical relationship with spirit—the animating, dynamic, sacred principles within all things and beyond. And we have found this sort of spiritual pursuit to lend richness, wonder, and meaning to our lives.

Spirituality in Motion

It is one thing to give an intellectual assent to the ideas and practices outlined in this book. But will you do the work? Witchery is a practice. But, if you are currently more of a reader than a doer, please don't be put off. We are all constantly growing in our practice, no matter how experienced, and it is always possible for a witch to start small (or big) and cultivate a deeply meaningful practice for themselves.

In order to identify and develop perceptions of the sacred and the many influences at work in ourselves and our environment, we need both study and practice. Once a practitioner has actually experienced something that they learned or formed in study, it takes on new life and deeper meaning unique to that individual. Without study, we may not be inspired to practice with depth; without practice, we cannot fully understand our study.

As you continue on your journey of cultivating a dynamic spiritual practice, you will integrate or release aspects of previous spiritual practice depending on how effective they are at enabling you to experience your relationship with the sacred now. You are the authority on what works specifically for you. But it's good to remember that easy is not the same as working, and difficult doesn't always indicate a mismatch. You are responsible for your spiritual path, and that path will grow and change as you grow and change.

Although I have written of some slightly abstract ideological underpinnings in this chapter, your spirituality is not a matter of abstraction as a witch. It is a matter for the nitty gritty of your life, and the shape it takes is uniquely yours. By various means, however eccentric, we carve niches to celebrate the spirits that fill our lives; we savor and cultivate connected moments in our busy days; and we open ourselves to the wonder and the holy terror of mystery.

As you continue through this book, each chapter will be useful in developing a different practical aspect of traditional witchcraft. A good general place to start is by assessing your current magical practices, their origins, and how well they work for you. Not all day-to-day spiritual practices are formal or complex. While you may rise at dawn to make offerings at an altar, you may also, almost without recognizing it as spiritual, take a regular moment to see and know a tree you pass on your commute. Some will be drawn to more formal work, while others may be able to maintain regularity with more spontaneous connection, but most of us will find a balance somewhere in between.

Reflection

1. What was the religious tradition of your childhood, and how do you think it influences your approach to witchcraft?

2. What appeals to you about this book so far? What beliefs, practices, and values resonate with you?

3. What most appeals to you about your own spiritual practice? How does it (or how do you envision it will) add to your quality of life, change you, or make you a witch?

4. Which connection do you most need to strengthen? The connections with yourself, gods, nature spirits, the ancestors, the community, or other? What means might you use to strengthen those relationships? What means might be effective in growing or further developing those connections? What do you think the greatest obstacles are to cultivating those connections further?

2

COMMUNING
WITH SPIRITS

Witches feel spirit connection in their bones. The lure of the crow on the rooftop, the ancient god, the beach rock, the long-dead great uncle, the whisper in the woods are powerful for us. It feels important, even before we have words to describe the experience. That heart-tug is a recognition of another being offering a greeting. It holds the beginning of a connection, a potential for partnership. Spirit work is how we deepen those first stirrings to create a working relationship. The being on the other side of that relationship is sometimes called an ally.

This chapter is the practical, general advice for the witch who is looking to build relationships with any number of categories of spiritual beings. For a witch, the term *spirits* can imply any number of entities in—or very commonly straddling—categories. The importance of the spirits of nature are discussed at length in the chapter Green and Local Witchcraft, while ancestors are introduced in Spiritual Ancestry, and working with gods is discussed in Theology. All of those concepts and relationships are significant ways of working with spirits.

The Importance of Communion

This chapter is called Communing with Spirits because the act of communion is a powerful and multifaceted idea that can help define our relationships with others. Communion is the act of sharing; it is a mutual relationship. A communion refers to a related body of persons who share things in common. It conveys the importance of relationship and community and deepens the concept of spirit work with a sense of spiritual togetherness.

If I ask, with no context, how do you make friends with others, chances are good that most people will think immediately of human to human friendships. So let's use our collective tendency toward human-centeredness to create an analogy for spirit work. Not all humans want to be your friend. Many won't share your interests, goals, or values. There are probably people who can't tolerate your quirks, and you can't tolerate theirs. You can be respectful of the existence of those people without needing to form a deeper relationship with them. So it is for the kinds of person who are not living humans. Some people are worse than incompatible or disinterested, they are hostile, violent, and hateful. Some people are only work friends, and some are friendly for a while but drift away. If you're lucky, some friends are like family. They are forever friends, and you are there for each other through thick and thin. So it is with spirits.

No friend wants to feel used. To feel that someone only accepts you for what you can give them—connections, status, material things—is a hollow, icky feeling. And yet, exchange is part of relationships. Your friends help you move and you cook them a special meal. The exchanges are there, but they're the *result* of a mutual relationship. It is very easy for witchcraft to drift toward a hollow, user kind of relationship. What can that plant do for me? What protection will that god give me?

We are, of course, given useful help, lessons, skills, and understandings by our spirit allies. And we also give of ourselves to them. But seeing them—really seeing them—and appreciating their nature underlies all gifts given and received. So, all this is to say that witches of the Forest's Edge do not *use* spirits. Whether the beings in question are plants, animals, deceased humans, or sundry Other Folk, we work in partnership with other-than-human persons. We build relationships over time with respectful, mutual intention and attention. Not only does the effort toward communion make for a more powerful, practical witchery, but also being consistent and intentional about relationship building with Others can be a foundational and transformative spiritual practice for the ever-developing witch.

The Trouble with Categories

I mentioned above that spirits are prone to straddle categories, and this can make speaking or writing about them difficult. Many spirits are liminal beings and perhaps that's why witches, also liminal creatures, traditionally have an association with them.

Witches interested in historical, religious, and anthropological research might enjoy looking more deeply into the complexity, diversity, and details of the often interwoven conceptualizations of the dead, the fae, familiars, nature spirits, angels, and demons in various cultures—especially with regard to those cultures in which you have individual spiritual ancestry. Depending upon your current geographical location and your own personal sense of ancestry, you will have (or eventually have) your own sense of what defines a given kind of spirit. Theological stances on the afterlife are apt to inform each witch's understanding, as are individual spiritual ancestry and culture. Keep in mind, though, that those persons who are not living humans are generally less obsessed with neat categories than are we. A multifaceted and ever-evolving understanding of the Others we encounter is by its nature imperfect and incomplete, but that complexity renders it no less powerful.

We have seen this shifting complexity in history when Christianity has taken over a region, and sometimes local gods become blended with saints. Or, a ghost attached to a natural feature can come to be revered as a nature spirit. Many witches regard the ancient gods as something akin to their earliest ancestors, and the most powerful dead as something akin to gods.

Fairies, a perennially popular topic among witches, offer an excellent example of change and complexity in categorization. While many cultures have beings that could be considered fairy-like, Britain and Ireland have an interesting trove of fairy lore. Beginning variously as diminished gods, nature spirits, and most commonly the human dead, fairies became associated with demons thanks to the influence of Puritan Christianity, and with angels thanks to less stringent forms of Christianity. Playing a starring role in British witchcraft trials, fairies only became the cute and mild winged creatures we recognize from childhood when the industrialization of the Victorian and Edwardian eras made people yearn for romantic symbols of a simpler time. Fairies are the ultimate category crossers!

A Process for Forging New Connections

These general steps can be applied to work with any kind of spirit.

1. **First, take stock.** Identify the calling or intention behind the relationship you want to explore. Note what spirit work you already feel drawn to explore. More often than not you'll know.

Those beings who want to work with you are already calling you. Sometimes their call is gentle and other times the call is rather more like a smack upside the head. You just have to listen and respond respectfully. Take stock of ways you are already pursuing that relationship—and be sure to give yourself credit for everything no matter how small you might think it is.

2. **Cultivate understanding.** Read, discuss, reflect. See what your ancestral cultures have to say. See what traditions and preferences certain beings are thought to have in folklore and tradition. See what fellow witches do, and listen to your own intuition. Divination can be used to ask different spirits how they would like to work with you.

3. **Make space for the relationship to flourish.** In your heart, in your home, and in your witchcraft. Develop rich imagery and sensory connections. Depending on your own preferences, this might involve forming mental images of the spirits involved, collecting or creating physical representations, writing descriptions of what the spirit is like, identifying scents, music, sensations that resonate with your chosen spirits.

4. **Give, before expecting to receive.** While you are reading, reflecting, and forming images of your spirits, begin a regular practice by making simple offerings. Make them frequently. Offerings need not be fancy or highly ceremonial, but they should be pretty consistent and ideally often enough that it does impact your life somewhat and becomes part of its fabric. "Only when you think of it," is too easy. Being a spiritworker is, well, work. Making offerings is a key way of showing hospitality and building a relationship gradually.

5. **Listen and try to be open to receive return communication.** Observe the world around you and take notice of things that are meaningful or related to your new ally. Maybe when you make an offering you sense the spirit's presence distinctly. Maybe you find certain bits of insight or creativity springing more easily to mind. If you're doubting the reciprocity of the relationship and have made a good faith effort to connect, turn to divination for guidance. Ask the ally to communicate through an open-ended reading or to confirm that they are interested in working with you.

6. **Receive with gratitude.** And accept the honor of working with allies. Focus on the sense of connectedness through time and space. You are ready to invite the new ally into your usual ritual space when you feel a beginning sense of connection and have begun to notice reciprocity. It does not require feeling that you are some kind of super-expert historian, theologian, ecologist, folklorist, or that your sense of connection is complete. (In fact, like all relationships, this one is ever evolving and being renegotiated.)

With these basic guidelines, your practice is pretty well begun. Open yourself to the teachings of those who work with you. Go where you are called, and your own path with the spirits will unfold. If you are still having trouble feeling connected and moving forward, a couple of things are likely from my experience with apprentices: 1) You are trying to work with spirits you think are appropriate for some external reason, not those to whom your heart is drawn or those who are reaching out to you. Or 2) You are really struggling to trust yourself, your intuition, and your experience enough to be open to receiving connection. In which case, it might be more meaningful for you to do some inner work to know and trust yourself before trying to reach out to the other-than-human community. Working closely with a very nurturing deity may also be healing in this case.

A Few Techniques for Establishing and Maintaining Communion

The following techniques are listed in alphabetical order, apart from offerings. The practice of giving offerings is fundamental, both in terms of day-to-day practice and as a starting point for beginners. Many of the other practices would commonly be preceeded by, followed by, or combined with offerings.

- **Offerings:** These are mentioned above and are a practice that is both fundamental and almost infinitely variable. Consider the preferences and traditions of the entities and associated cultures, and work with the many items, locations, timings, and other options that are available. Quite possibly the most popular offering through time and across multiple cultures is food and drink. Anything you can create or own can be an offering, and they can be buried, burned, thrown into a body of water, left outdoors, or placed on an altar.

  Offerings can also be indirect. Offerings of money or volunteer time are common and wonderful. Hecate is said to like offerings in her name at food pantries. Spirits associated with wildness might enjoy donations to conservation groups or the orchestration of a clean-up event. Money donations often allow you to enter a name that the gift is in honor of. That is a great opportunity to state clearly that it is in honor of your ally.

  Witches in our tradition are diverse in our offering practices in part because we work with diverse entities for diverse purposes. Groups and individuals generally use offerings as part of moving into liminal space during ritual and for establishing hospitable, reciprocal connections, rather like inviting friends to gather around our hearth with a tasty beverage and a bite to eat.

- **Art:** All forms of art and craft can be used mindfully to honor and connect with spirits. The physical process of creation in any medium can help you process and viscerally integrate your understanding of your spirit. Art can be shared or entirely private, but showing others your vision of a being can create a gratifying and clarifying experience.

- **Divination:** Of course you can interact with sundry entities through divinatory tools. You may find that some tools are more appropriate to working with certain entities or that certain entities will speak only though some tools. Divination is commonly used to see if an important offering has been accepted.

- **Dreams:** Sundry spirits will spontaneously make contact through dreams, or intentional contact can be requested.

- **Holy Places:** Visiting, caring for, making offerings at, or otherwise acknowledging special places beloved or inhabited by spirits can help establish and maintain connection whether the holy place is a tree, a stone circle, a gravesite, a well, a church, or your back garden.

- **Intuitive Contact:** Sometimes things just happen, and you just know. Some messages from your spirits will arrive in your mind or body without any intermediary. If this appeals to you, you can request this kind of contact.

- **Mirrors:** Ceremonial magic popularized the practice of calling entities into dark mirrors in order to interact with them. Many witches adopt and adapt this practice for our own purposes. Indeed, any substance or surface used for scrying can be a medium for invoking a spirit.

- **Possession, Meditation, and Hedgecrossing:** In fact, any practice that involves altered states of consciousness can be a method for interacting with spirits. One of the more obvious is ritual possession, often called *drawing down* when referring to deity work with goddesses.

- **Ritual and Devotional Elements:** Repeated ritual elements, from invocations to meditations to offerings, invite and maintain contact.

- **Spirit Houses:** In the broad sense, this refers to a physical object that both represents the spirit or type of spirit and that the spirit can inhabit or be called into either permanently or temporarily. A spirit house can be a small clay house, a jar, a feather, a bone, a skull, or other object.

Dangerous Liaisons

Not all spirits are friendly, and witches are wise to be mindful of that, although there is no need for paranoia. Whether you have crossed into the Otherworld or have invited contact in our reality, a few guidelines will serve you well.

1. **Be very clear in your intentions.** For example, if you say pretty words but are really just seeking a thrill, be aware that there are things out there that will gladly give you far more than the little thrill you were seeking. Be careful with your words. Some things can be taken more than one way and you may encounter tricky Folk inclined to do just that.

2. **Employ your intuition.** Feel for the authentic core of the being in question. Other-than-human spirit beings are often not bound by physical form. This tends to be most true of those beings encountered while hedgeriding but can also be the case here. Do not make assumptions based on appearance. Rely instead on your sense of the entity's core being or energy signature. Keep in mind that, like humans, many spirit people can also hide their true intentions, play tricks, and lie.

3. **Be in a good space.** This can be physical, mental, emotional, and spiritual. Your inner strength, self-trust, intuition, logic, and resilience are powerful tools. More literally, the presence of fellow witches, the use of a warded space, and ritual tools are also powerful and likely to be particularly important for less experienced witches.

4. **Request and accept help and guidance.** Once you have formed relationships with relatively stable spirits, you will be more secure in more adventuresome contacts. For example, patron deities, benevolent ancestors, familiars, angelic beings, egregores, and some animal guides, can be invaluable guardians for you as you venture further afield. You could, for example, ask a patron deity for a sign that a certain entity is who they says they are, or ask a familiar to hedgecross with you and give

a warning as needed. You could also ask a familiar spirit to guard your body while your soul is flying. Guardianship and guidance can also come from your fellow witches.

It is very rare, but possible, to attract the persistent, invasive attention of a malevolent entity. Dealing with that situation is more or less what people mean by an exorcism. This is not a one size-fits-all kind of situation and does not have one solution. If you are ever concerned about dealing with more than you can handle, reach out to experienced witches in your community.

Reflection

1. Can you remember when you were first able to sense and interact with other-than-human spirits?

2. How experienced do you consider yourself as a spiritworker?

3. Are there particular categories of spirit that resonate or feel easy to you? Any that feel like more of a stretch?

4. What are your current thoughts about who the fae are? Where does this understanding come from—is it associated with a particular culture? Author? Experience? How might you continue to develop this understanding?

5. What are familiars? Are there different kinds? Do you work with familiars? Where does this understanding come from—is it associated with a particular culture, text, or direct experience? How might you continue to develop this understanding?

Practice

- Use a combination of the techniques suggested in this material to build or expand a spirit allyship. (But in truth, most of the practices suggested in this book put these principles to use.)

3

SPIRITUAL ANCESTRY

Much of your deepest magic is born of your ancestors, just as you are. You come from a long line of powerful healers, creators, storytellers, spirit workers, and herbalists. Your ancestors are in the billions, spread across the globe and through eons. Your roots are deep and wide. The very marrow of your bones holds history full of wonders. The electric synapses of your brain whisper the words of teachers, ghosts, friends, and guides who have left our world but whose ideas live in you. This is true of you because it is true of all of us. You stand in a tremendously powerful river's current of blood, love, life, and death.

The concept of spiritual ancestry holds an important place in witchcraft at the Forest's Edge. We honor the ancestors as those who came before us in a spiritual if not necessarily biological sense, and we draw inspiration and practices from them. Instead of picking up bits and pieces from this or that arbitrary source, grounding your practice in ancestry grabs hold of your true roots. In this sense, every witch has a lineage, because by blood and spirit, we have ancestors who can speak to us of magic. This concept is woven throughout this book as it is absolutely fundamental to authentic traditional witch-craft. Like local ecology, ancestry influences the specifics of our crafts from how we use divination to how we work spells. Exploring the specifics of your ancestry is work that can bring profound rewards. Each witch is a molecule in a great river of lives and deaths, and the trick of ancestral magic is to let the whole river run through you.

Ancestors of Blood

Your ancestors of blood are the folks with whom you typically share the ties of genes. This is the family you're born into, the leaves on your family tree. This is the first, or maybe only, kind of ancestor that comes to mind for most people. Perhaps you are one of the many witches who uses the magical power of Internet research to learn about your recent ancestors. Maybe you know your people going back a couple of generations or hundreds of years. Whether you know a lot or a little, some of these ancestors long for a deeper connection with you. If you have an established practice of ancestor veneration, you know this. There's nothing quite like the help and guidance of your ancestors. It's a different relationship than you can share with a plant spirit or deity. Ancestors can root for you in such a personal way, with all the fire and force of human care and emotion. Your ancestors' investment in you, personally, as part of their lineage is a special gift.

This also applies to ancestry for adoptees. The nature of adoption in this culture is that it is a way of making a person a blood relative. Adopted children have all the legal rights and responsibilities of a biological child. Spiritually, this includes the right of ancestor veneration, if they so choose. Adoptive families can be considered ancestors of blood. Each adoptee decides for themselves how and if to venerate biological and adoptive ancestors.

Another aspect of recent, traceable ancestry that is typically relevant for a witch is a general pattern of migration and ethnic or geographical origin. You could call this a sort of macro-ancestry. The specific individuals in your family tree connect you to whole cultures and regions. Most folks have a few dominant ancestral identities to which they feel drawn. There is nothing wrong with embracing ancestors born on another continent, whatever your current identity. Indeed, it is wonderful! One path to growth as an ancestral witch is to deepen your understanding of those cultures, including through non-Pagan sources. A deep dive into the history, anthropology, and folklore of your ancestral origins can be ever so powerful in pushing your craft further.

Shifting to a smaller, more personal micro-scale, your very recent ancestry is also worth exploring. Perhaps your grandparents hail from a particular state or region within your country. Does that region have folktales? Songs? History? You bet it does! And, as a witch reaching for your deepest roots, that can be a delightful direction. Perhaps there were sayings or superstitions passed along in your family that can point to the ways folk magical practices weave through all our lineages. By way of example, one of my grandfathers was a New England sailor, who, when deciding whether we should sail the next day would tell me, "red sky at night, sailor's delight; red in the morning, sailors take warning." I discovered through a book of New England folklore that this rhyme comes from a longer one detailing a variety of weather-related signs and omens—an interesting find for a nature witch. When you find a source from one nugget of ancestral lore, more are likely to be found, whether from a person or a book.

Most of us live in multicultural societies and each individual witch likely has multiple threads of ancestry that have been woven together through time and space to create you. Connecting seriously with your ancestry is a way to make your craft truly your own, specific to your combination of cultural influences and your identity.

Ancestors of Spirit

If you listened in to my rituals, you would commonly hear the phrase "ancestors of blood and spirit" or something quite like it, so let's turn to the less familiar but equally important kind of ancestry. Not all ancestors are genetic or legally adopted relatives. Your spiritual ancestors can be those folks who claim you and whom you claim—whoever they are. In our tradition, members share some common spiritual ancestry, and each individual also has their own unique sense of ancestry. You might have spiritual ancestors who were mentors, role models, or family friends. You might have ancestors who had any number of roles and identities that resonate for you. Your ancestors of spirit might come through a community, religious tradition, or meaningful profession. For some witches it can feel more difficult to identify with non-relatives as ancestors, while for others it is actually easier or more comfortable. However you choose to balance your work with different types of ancestors, they all have a role in shaping the unique kind of witch that you are.

Many witches claim magical practitioners as spiritual ancestors. History contains many kinds of magic workers going by many different names, from an auntie whose prayers to a folk saint are known as especially effective to a village elder of a time long past who mediated between people and spirits. Magical ancestors need not embrace the title *witch* to be willing to work with you, although some may indeed have embraced it. In my tradition, Isobel Gowdie, a Scottish witch, whom some modern witches got to know through the discoveries and analysis of Emma Wilby, is a broadly held ancestor whose detailed confessions at her witchcraft trial have fascinated and enticed many modern readers, from practitioners to academics.

A personal ancestor of mine is a well-known granny midwife from the Appalachians, and while some of my blood ancestors also hail from those mountains, I do not believe she is blood kin to me. She never would have called herself a witch and as it was for many lay or granny midwives in the 19th and early 20th century, Christian faith was not at odds with her folkloric charms and healing traditions that we might call magic.

Your own spiritual ancestors may also be well outside the realm of witchcraft, and even apart from any form of folk magic. A knitter might find ancestry among fiber workers of the past. An activist might find ancestors among earlier activists. You may even find that spiritual ancestors who seem unrelated to magic can point you to the folkways of their time and place, so that you can find the enchantments hidden within. The only rules in identifying spiritual ancestors are that you feel a connection to them, and that they accept that claim of connection from you. If that sounds a bit daunting, refer back to the Communing with Spirits chapter and the veneration section below.

Ancestors of Prehistory

One thing that is sometimes easy to forget, especially for those of us immersed in family tree research, is the fact that the vast majority of all of our ancestry is prehistoric. This is to say that hours of genealogical research yield only the tiniest fraction of a percent of your actual ancestors. That doesn't render it meaningless—far from it! But rather I want you to feel inspired by the tremendous wealth of pre-industrial, pre-agricultural, and prehistoric ancestors that you have beyond the reach of genealogical research. There can be a freedom found in reaching back beyond your current societal and cultural context.

Considering this truth also reminds us of our connections with all other humans because at some point, no matter how far back, we all share a common human family line. As with all deeper research, you can go straight to relevant disciplines like history and anthropology. That does not, however, mean you always have to search out dense, arcane texts. A comfy starting place could be documentaries available online or on digital streaming services. As a homeschooling parent, I am unashamed to admit that a good deal of my knowledge of prehistoric humans comes from resources meant for school children. As long as the resources are up to date, this can be an excellent, and often visual, starting point for exploration.

Ancestors of Community and Tradition

Ancestral work has a curious effect of both highlighting your uniqueness while also uniting you with others who share *aspects* of their ancestry in common with you. This can hold true for families and communities of culture and identity, of course. It also holds true for groups of witches who choose to gather together with a common bond.

In our tradition, each witch is encouraged and supported to continuously develop their own specific sense of ancestry and to determine whether it communes, at least in part, with the existing spiritual ancestry shared by the tradition. This is just how we do things, but if you are considering joining or forming any community of witches, consider shared ancestry as one means for discerning your sense of the group.

Ancestor Trouble

Maybe some of your ancestry is shrouded by slavery or closed adoption, or perhaps it is complicated by family traumas. Sometimes the trauma, whether societal or personal, is so great that connecting with blood ancestry is fraught. In that case, it typically works best to focus at first on some aspect of blood or spiritual ancestry that feels empowering and supportive. Those supportive ancestors can then become allies if you eventually choose to approach the more challenging parts of your family tree.

Embracing and exploring cultures in your ancestry does not mean ignoring the negative aspects of those cultures. Whatever geographies, cultures, religions, and folk traditions you hail from, chances are good that some of them did some seriously bad stuff. Digging into your ancestry requires an honest look into that pain and a willingness to grapple with those realities, without either minimizing atrocities or tossing out a whole culture because something is problematic.

In my experience, one issue that sometimes crops up, especially when exploring recent, biological ancestry, is the issue of ancestors being brought into witchy practices when in life those same ancestors might have rejected any notion of witchcraft and may have disapproved of it vehemently. Not all recent ancestors will have held these views, and many may recognize their practices in yours, but some might. I find it can often be the case that the dead have a broader and less linear view of things. Their urge to help and strengthen their lineage can sometimes trump earthly religious divides. It is often the case that their broader view includes a shared love of family, land, animals, work, teaching, and the like. And a person who would have reacted badly to any mention of witchcraft in life may now be able to work with you as a healer or a parent or whatever it is that you are and are doing. Perhaps they even see that their superstitions in life are a thread that ties into your work as a witch.

I cannot tell you what a specific ancestor of yours thinks, but you can certainly find out. First, if you're not sure, ask! Use intuition, dreams, divination, and the acceptance of offerings. If you feel that Great-Grandpa Carlos is hostile, standoffish, and generally saying, "No!" then back off. You have plenty of other folks to work with.

A second issue is the issue of recent ancestors who are, quite frankly, at the very least jerks, and, at worst, perpetrators of crimes and trauma. If this is a consideration for you, just know that you are far from alone. Quite frankly, they are dead, and you are a witch, and now *you* get to choose. If your ancestor altar is like your dining table, then you are the host who decides who is welcome at the table. A common and easy way to do this at first is to verbalize that only those ancestors who come in a spirit of love and goodwill (or whatever language you favor) are invited, and mean it.

And finally, you, the living witch, have such tremendous power in your relationship with ancestors that you can not only choose which ancestors are invited, but also, if you like, you can work to help those ancestors who are more troubled or troublesome. This practice can take many forms and is sometimes called *ancestor elevation* or *intergenerational healing*. In the simplest form, even if you choose never to deal directly with troubled ancestors, you might leave special offerings to help heal past harms in your lineage.

After death, it is possible for the spirit of a person to continue to grow and change. Experienced spirit workers know this because we have seen it, and sometimes because we have actively worked to bring it about. While it is possible to occasionally and superficially acknowledge your ancestors, witches of our sort eventually strive to go deeper, whenever we are ready in our hearts and skillsets. We use the witchy tools at our disposal, such as divination, intuition, ritual, offerings, hedgecrossing, spellwork, dream incubation, and possession to gradually deepen and personalize our work with these spirits.

For many of us, this ultimately entails a personal and profound realization not only of how much love and power flows through our bloodlines but also of how much grief, pain, oppression, dysfunction, and trauma flows across generations. A reality of working deeply with ancestors is eventually getting to the hard part. The practical reality of having a whole lot of ancestors is that they have done all the good things you want for yourself, and also the darker things that you wish were not true. Perhaps you are holding untapped grief for someone more recent who has died, or as is often the case, both grief and anger. Or perhaps there are legacies of mental illness, abuse, oppression, imprisonment, or other human experiences that have left a mark on your family line. Maybe you have had so many positive familial relationships in this life that it feels like a betrayal to look hard at the tougher aspects. Digging into these challenging aspects of ancestry is one of the practices that falls under the concept of shadow work.

What we know is that it *all* matters. The glorious and the excruciating. We know that whole witches are the most effective. So all of this ancestral stuff matters whether or not it even happened to you, the living witch. Science has only just begun to study the effects of fear, trauma, and famine passed down to subsequent generations, and so far their results are compelling. Some psychotherapists have even begun doing work with ancestors to address intergenerational trauma. But as witches, we know this in our bones—digging into both sides is the most profound way to tap into our power.

Ancestry in Practice—Veneration

Having covered the types of ancestry, let's address what witches actually *do* with that ancestry. When I talk of honoring and working with ancestors, what I mean is that we witches are participating in a long line of people who practice ancestor veneration. Archeological finds suggest that even the forerunners of modern humans may have engaged in ancestor veneration. I use the word "veneration" instead of worship because the word "worship" carries a connotation of adoring reverence for a deity, most commonly a monotheistic God. I approach ancestors with a spirit of partnership and a desire to foster a mutually beneficial relationship, just as I approach other spirits with whom I work. The same principles of building a relationship apply whether the spirits you are addressing are ancestral, fae, or natural. The general steps to building a relationship are laid out in the previous chapter, so I will apply them here as an example.

First, take stock of what you are already doing. Even a less experienced witch may find more ancestor veneration than they expect. Perhaps you leave flowers on a loved one's grave, or maybe you have a wall with family photos, or maybe you have a sense that your grandfather is watching over your child. Perhaps in a tough spot you think of what your mentor would have done or maybe your grandmother's folk sayings echo in your ears as you go about your life. You are honoring, connecting, and building relationship even with these mainstream practices. It's a wonderful starting place.

Second, make room for your invited ancestors—in your heart, your thoughts, your home, and your ritual practices. The most common way to start is by creating an ancestor altar in your home and also ensuring that some sort of ancestral representation (physical or verbal) enters into your other ritual spaces. The ancestor representation for other spaces can be anything you chose. A replica human skull is typically used in my tradition, but a purpose-made *poppet* can work just as well.

Begin to reach out your intuitive senses to feel the presence of your ancestors when you welcome them. This may feel odd and ineffective at first, but keep at it on a very regular basis and in time it

The Witch at the Forest's Edge

will click. At an emotional level, beginning with ancestral work can involve an inner shift to create space in your heart to truly connect. For some this can be difficult due to fears around death and loss or because of the effects of challenging family relationships. If you are just beginning an ancestral practice, start with ancestors you experience as warm and uncomplicatedly benevolent. You may know of those people by name, or you may only intuitively sense or visualize them. These ancestors can become fast allies who can support and anchor your future ancestral work.

Must an ancestor altar be so dark or witchy that an outsider would always perceive them as such? No! I am all for the darkly witchy, but my ancestor altar is in my frequently used family dining room. I love having my ancestors right there when gathering with family and friends for a meal. My spouse and kids know what it is, of course, but to others it is typically unremarkable. Shrouding your work in subtlety makes it no less powerful. Your ancestors no doubt understand the possible dangers of overt witchcraft.

Third, give before expecting to receive. Making room begins a process of offering hospitality and honor to your ancestors. You might continue that process by making an offering of intention by spending time at the altar, or an offering of intellect by researching the professions, time periods, cultures, or causes that relate to your ancestors. In addition, regular physical offerings of water or any other relevant substance is like refilling the cups of your guests. Dark (or new) moons and, of course, Samhain are excellent times for regular ancestor work.

Fourth, listen and receive the benefits of a reciprocal relationship with your beloved dead. As your relationship develops, you will be able to sense their support when you reach for it and tap into their power for ritual work. All the sorts of witches' work can draw on ancestors—from divination to hedgeriding to spellwork to to connect and a treasure trove of ancestral lore. Some family members may be uncomfortable being recorded. At times it can work best to chat casually and then write down what you learned soon after.

- Name your lineage. Work though your influences and consider whose voices have called you to where you are today. How do you see yourself as being called to and formed in the path of witchery? Trace the lines of your ancestors, feeding into who you are now. Any ancestors—of blood and spirit, individual and communal, named and unnamed—can be included. The final product could be a narrative description of your roots as witch, a visual family tree, mind map, or flowchart—whichever best suits your way of thinking. At times the idea of a family line of witches or having named lineage via an organized tradition is held up as a separate and even superior way of being a witch. In truth we all have a lineage. This is an opportunity to creatively describe yours.

- If you are not already working with your own ancestors on a practical level, develop an individualized plan to forge a relationship. Review the material on Spiritual Ancestry and Communing with Spirits as needed. If you do have a close, working ancestral relationship, find your growing edge and work with that. If pushing further into this realm feels frightening, then be present with that. But still do it, even if afraid. The liminal spaces where witches work are often dark, uncertain, and laced with potential failure. Go there.

4

INTUITION

Intuition is an ability to acquire knowledge or understanding without conscious use of analytical reasoning. But—and this is where so many folks get hung up—intuition does not emerge from a vacuum. It seems to arise suddenly from within us, but, in fact, intuition has many sources, such as prior experience, factual knowledge, unconscious biases, sensory input, observation, and divine or Otherworldly influence, as well as from within the sacred core of the witches themselves.

A few examples of intuition's external sources:

A witch well-versed in folk herbalism decides to intuitively choose plants to work with for a spell. They will work with the plants that come readily to mind, even if they seem surprising, because their knowledge of medicinal and magical plant lore will subconsciously inform their choice.

Another witch buys a new pack of oracle cards, and the first card shows a sunflower. They intuitively know that this card signifies warmth, joy, and youth. This intuition is partially informed by their positive memories of growing sunflowers with their grandmother and cultural conventions around sun, the color yellow, and sunflowers.

A third witch has tea with a friend who says they're feeling fine, but the witch knows intuitively that's not true. One source of that intuition, whether the witch consciously noted it or not, is that the friend was twisting their wedding ring and looking away.

Putting Intuition to the Test

Although witches work closely with intuition and value it highly, intuition often has an awkward outcome, namely beliefs we may not be able to justify. Discerning the difference between true intuition and just wanting something to be true so badly that we ascribe it to intuition can be tough. The examples offered above are positive and benign, but when an intuitive sense carries significant consequences, it can become especially important to look at it carefully. One way to examine an intuited notion is to consider it from three perspectives: reason, tradition, and experience.

Reason

What does my analytical side say about this?

Just because intuition does not come from conscious reasoning doesn't mean you can't use your innate reasoning ability after the fact. This means thinking rationally about your intuitive conclusion. Be introspective. Consider the sources that contributed to your intuition. Consider the consequences. Are there any unconscious biases at play? Does it align with your values?

Tradition

What does my community say about this?

You may choose to check your intuition with the teachings of a group you're a part of or against writings found in relevant books and articles. It can also mean talking it over with your teacher or other witches. Tradition can also refer to your friends and family and to the values you hold in common with them. It can mean comparing it to the beliefs, cultural context, and values of your spiritual ancestors or the pagan and witchcraft communities more broadly.

Experience

What does my life experience say about this?

How does this intuition fit into the larger story of your life? Does it align well with what you have already learned and experienced in your path? Then, as far as your immediate experience, what is it like for you to have this intuition? Does it feel good? Painful? Challenging?

Keep in mind that seeming illogical, idiosyncratic, or painful doesn't mean an intuition isn't true for you. This is just a way to consider your intuition from multiple perspectives, but the outcome of this discernment process is yours alone.

Intuition and Witchcraft

When witches talk about "trusting your intuition," we are emphasizing how important it is to avoid immediately dismissing ideas and perceptions that seem to "just come to you." Those intuitive notions can have very valid sources, both internal and external, and can have a meaningful and inspiring impact on your practice, if you are able to trust them. Intuition is a key way for the spirits we work with to communicate with us. The more attention you pay to intuition, the more intuitive you can become. You cultivate the raw materials of intuition during your work as a witch by building your experience, your knowledge, your observational skills, and your relationship with spirits. This increases your trust in yourself and your willingness to hear your intuitive truths.

A few ways witches apply intuition:

- We use it to create new rituals that are moving and effective

- We make on-the-fly decisions and substitutions in spells, potions, offerings, and incense blends

- We help and heal using a sense of what plants, animals, and people may need

- We do divination

Most importantly, we come to believe our own spiritual promptings enough to follow them into deeper experiences. When we are bold enough to attend to our intuition by listening carefully to all sorts of inner and outer promptings, the world becomes more magical, more richly enspirited with signs, whispers, and meaning.

Reflection

1. Reflecting on the material presented here, but using your own words, define intuition.

2. Give an example of a time you have used your intuition in the past month.

channeling. At each ritual, regardless of the purpose—at least any that are formal enough to be called a ritual—I call upon my ancestors as powerful allies.

After all, as spirits go, the people of your own line are likely to be the most personally invested in your wellbeing. In time, you may find that stepping into this river of blood is transformative and letting their power flow through you is a deep enchantment.

Reflection

1. Notice the feelings that come up for you when you hear the language of ancestry and family. Is your first impression the warmth of love? A surge of pride? A sense of unease? A stab of shame? Or maybe it's complicated.

2. What obstacles do you expect to encounter as you take a next step to either begin or deepen your ancestral practices?

3. What is the most enticing aspect of ancestor veneration for you? Where's your starting point or how might you deepen your work?

4. How does working with ancestors intersect with your views on the afterlife?

Practice

- Interview a family member about songs and sayings they remember from growing up. Collecting family history and lore, without necessarily mentioning magic, can be both a way

3. Is tapping into your intuition difficult for you, or easy? Has it always been that way?

4. What goal would you choose to set for yourself to continue to cultivate or refine your intuitive abilities?

Practice

- The best way to develop your intuition is to listen for it, acknowledge it, test it, and use it—over and over. Intuition is like a muscle that grows stronger with exercise.

- Carry a small journal with you and keep an eye out for your intuitions. Jot them down. In the beginning, you might not have very many written down, but they will likely increase in number and strength in time as you become attuned to noticing them.

- Consider the ways that witches use intuition in their craft. Choose an aspect of your own practice and try a purely intuitive approach (perhaps in writing a spell or interpreting tarot cards, for example). Record the work and how it felt to be guided in your craft by intuition.

- Ground and center yourself in a relaxed state. Have a pencil and paper ready. Focus on the question, "What do I need in my life right now?" Mindfully ask that question (aloud or silently) three times. Ask slowly, feeling it become more meaningful with each query. When you're ready, write or draw the first thing that comes to mind. It could result in anything from a word, to a collection of simple shapes, to a recognizable drawing. Intuitively interpret its meaning. Does your interpretation feel right? Try to consider the sources of information that informed your intuition.

- Set aside some time to go for a solitary walk or a drive in an unfamiliar area. Start walking or driving without knowing where you are going. Resist the urge to follow the first few ideas about where to go that seem to come from your mind offering *shoulds* and *coulds*. Focus on the sensations of your body. Go in the direction that makes your body feel relaxed, grounded, and good. If you feel your awareness becoming primarily verbal, analytical, and mental again, gently re-focus on the sensations of your body. Your body is your intuitive compass for this experimental journey, so keep following those pleasant, relaxed sensations. (Just a note, those with unresolved trauma histories may have special challenges with being *in* their bodies as this exercise suggests. Only do what is right for you.)

5

CULTIVATING
SPIRIT SENSES

Spirit senses are the sort of senses that are sometimes described by terms like visualization, imagery, imagination, or the mind's eye. Most of these terms emphasize only sight, while witches work far more effectively with *all* the senses. It's true that sight is the dominant sense for humans as a species, but the others are much more than an afterthought. Witches of the Forest's Edge hone their spirit senses as one of the keys to magic. Those senses can then be used to work magic in this world or in the Otherworld, to correctly perceive the spirits that are really there, and to alter our states of consciousness. We can create and open doors with our spirit senses, and as our work advances, the creations of our spirit senses become progressively more powerful.

You may be familiar with using ordinary senses in ritual and spellcraft. Perhaps you have worked with fresh herbs, incense, or essential oils to engage the sense of smell. Maybe you create statues or sigils or work with the imagery of tarot to draw on sight. Music, chanting, and incantation call on hearing. The feeling of ritual fabrics, shrouding, and fetish objects call on touch. Maybe you involve taste by toasting your spirits, sharing food offerings, or drinking ritual tea. Many things we do invoke multiple senses at once and often a particularly effective ritual or spell will work with them all.

The examples above of bodily senses in witchcraft are wonderful and important. They are also sensory experiences that most non-magical folks would be able to share. A random neighbor of mine could hear my death rattle and smell the pile of mugwort in the fire. These experiences seem to be entirely external and communal, but we know that they are not. We know from contemporary neuroscience that your eyes are not a camera. Your skin is not a touch pad. Your ears are not a microphone. You are far more complicated; and the liminal space between external reality and internal perception is huge, tangled, and largely unexplored. What we know is that there is simultaneous two-way communication between the brain and the sense organs.

It is, in fact, this give-and-take communion between brain and sense organs that creates what we understand as perception. Here is an example that can provide a bridge between mundane experience and the skills of witchery:

If I walk into my mother's house, my brain begins the process of perception with the expectation that I will see my mother. I am used to seeing my mother here. This is communicated to my eyes, and when I open the door and my retinas take in a shadowy silhouette of a bipedal shape of middling height backlit by an open window, I *know* that I am *seeing* my mother. However, my seeing began in my brain and was a result of a conversation between eye and brain. Now, substitute fairy, ancestor, or some other spirit for mother, and the witchy significance will become more clear.

So, as I write about spirit senses and ordinary senses, please know that I am making a distinction between them because language falls short of the wondrous reality of perception. The clear boundary exists only in words. The practice is, unsurprisingly, liminal. There is a very blurred line between what your jelly-filled globes see and what you can see with your mind's eye—between the image entering your retina and what you perceive.

Spirit Senses in Spellcraft

Witches use spirit senses in many aspects of spellcraft. Most of us with a bit of experience have done some of this, but expanding the sharpness of the senses and the ways we use them can be a powerful path even for a generally experienced witch. The creative power of our spirit senses is used to some extent in the casting of *all* spells, because seeing your desired outcome clearly is important for effectively directing your spell toward your intent. We use spirit senses in planning the work, visualizing the target, focusing and amplifying intent, using a visual device (like a sigil), sensing the magic moving to its target, and sensing the work of your spirit allies.

In fact, the use of sigils is another great example of the interface between ordinary senses and spirit senses in spellcraft. You use your ordinary sense of sight to create the sigil, and your sense of touch is activated by putting pen to paper to draw it. You may even notice the smells of ink and paper. This work with ordinary senses has the goal of carving the very essence of the sigil into your spirit senses, eventually drawing the shape so deeply into yourself that you do not need to be consciously visualizing it anymore to have it work its magic. In this case, the ordinary senses lead to the spirit senses, and ultimately beyond.

Although spirit sensing is part of all spellcraft, there are a couple more instances where it can be especially useful. When working magic upon a target at a distance, spirit senses can be deployed to foster the movement of the magic from the spellcaster to the target.

For example, let's say you were forcefully shooing a person out of your life. You might choose to shape the magic into a swarm of bees that you can see and hear as they travel from you to your target, delivering an uncomfortable sting to get your target moving away. A great advantage of using spirit sensing as a magical technique is that you can do it anywhere and any time, without need of any tools, ingredients, or physical space set aside for a working.

And, of course. it is entirely possible, typical, and very useful, to be able to combine both bodily senses and spirit senses in spell-work. Because rituals alter consciousness, it can be hard to discern between spirit senses and ordinary senses. In fact, in the best work-ings, the truth is revealed and experienced—that the distinction between those categories is closer to arbitrary than most would like to imagine.

Sensing Beyond

As you gain proficiency in using your spirit senses, being able to engage these senses with more clarity will become automatic. This can manifest in many ways. You may find yourself able to find lost things more easily or locate something in a broader environment—partially obscured herbs in the forest, for example. This is because you have heightened your ability to recognize what is real just beyond, beneath, and beside the obvious. Your clear sight may also manifest in your being able to see some things that are not available to everyone—you may spot a fey creature, a god's face, or magical barriers. You might also catch a bit of fragrance, feel a cool touch, or hear something no one else can, depending on your inherent intuitive strengths. Do not fear these developing abili-ties; simply treat them with the same process of observation and examination you would apply to any other information available to you. Respecting and paying attention to these abilities will allow them to flourish.

Spirit Senses in Hedgeriding

Among the many ways that witches use spirit sensing is as a tool pertaining to hedgeriding. Especially for the novice, comfort with spirit sensing can be an empowering stepping stone toward hedgeriding, which is the subject of a later chapter. Sometimes folks who are new to the practice of hedgeriding feel anxious about the difference between just imagining and really hedgeriding. Hopefully the explanation of spirit senses above makes it clear how perfectly unclear the mystery of perception is.

There is a whole spectrum of experience between just imagining and fully perceiving with the spirit senses, and those categories on either end of the spectrum are related, yet distinct. If the spectrum ranges from something that your conscious mind is conjuring (planned visualizations, for example) to something you perceive vividly but do not control (successful Otherworldly spirit flight), then the whole spectrum still requires the ability to use spirit senses.

Many witches begin hedgeriding by using some form of visualization or guided imagery. The reason for this is that it can cause a mindful relaxation in an anxious practitioner, but more importantly it puts the witch on one end of the spectrum. As the witch more fully imagines, employing their spirit senses, their place on the spectrum will often start to shift. Perhaps imperceptibly at first, but with practice the conscious use of spirit senses can create a doorway into truly experiencing other realms with all the senses.

Some Basic Instruction

Gaining strength in using your spirit senses is just like gaining physical strength or a knowledge-based proficiency—you have to do your exercises, practice, and be patient. Heightening your awareness of how you already successfully use them in your spellwork, for example, will help you to appreciate your real accomplishments and establish a starting point for further growth. As a simple early step, you might try looking at pictures and trying to recall them in detail or recalling the face of someone you haven't seen for a long time, then comparing your visualization to their photograph. But do not limit yourself to the sense of sight. Try to exactly recall a song in your mind, then play it for yourself to compare; hear the call of a certain bird or of a running creek. Concentrate on a certain smell until you can actually smell it, and the same with taste—start with the familiar, then challenge yourself. Try to innovate new ways you can employ spirit senses in your craft or the rest of your daily life. Make spirit sensing one of the most useful tools in your magical set.

Reflection

1. What do you think are your greatest challenges when it comes to working with spirit senses?

2. Can you think of any spell or piece of magic that you performed for which you didn't use any spirit senses? If so, what was the result?

3. Recall an experience when you saw, or thought you saw, something that wasn't there. Record the experience to the best

of your ability and then consider the possibility that you may have been seeing something with spirit sense. Why do you, or do you not, think this is likely?

4. When have you had trouble trusting something you saw, heard, or experienced out of the corner of your eye, in a meditation, or hedgeriding? Do you think your mistrust was a lack of faith in noncorporeal experiences, or were there other signs that you may have been simply imagining, dreaming, or there was a "trick of the light"?

Practice

- Sit somewhere comfortable and relax. Think back to a happy memory or a recent event. Immerse yourself in that memory. Try to remember every detail, and ask the following questions. What was the weather like? What were you wearing? Who was there? Can you remember any scents, sounds, or tastes?

- For those who take easily to visual spirit sensing but struggle to bring the other senses into the spiritual realm, begin with the ordinary versions of the other senses. Pay special attention to the scent, sounds, tastes, and feelings of your day-to-day life. As your mind wanders from this task, gently bring it back to focus. If this is too difficult, from time to time close your eyes and take note of the input from your other senses.

- Before visiting somewhere that you go often, take a few moments to recall one of your previous visits. When you arrive at the location, keep your recollection in mind and make some mental notes of any differences. Consider whether these differences are due to a lapse in memory, an objective change, or if they indicate something about the place energetically.

- Working with a partner, have one person leave the room. The remaining person silently invokes a spiritual presence. The person who left must detect what sort of being was invoked. Don't forget to thank those who were called after the exercise is done.

- Using all of your spirit senses, create a sacred space for yourself in as much detail as you can. Sit quietly and visualize this space on a regular basis. Each time you do this, record exactly what you heard, smelled, felt, tasted, or saw. After several visits, compare your records. Take note of any changes or evolutions, and consider whether they were of your making or outside your control. If this place becomes a place of importance and you feel it is in existence somewhere Other, be sure to energetically protect it when you go there, and to honor it and its gifts to you.

6

CREATING RITUAL

Witches' rituals are persuasive, hypnotic, sensory, and performative. They are deeply of this world and of our humanness. It is appropriately witchy that, for us, something so human and bodily becomes successful when through our most ordinary humanness we become more than human. Depending on the goal of the ritual, perhaps we shift into the form of a wild beast or lose our boundaries between self and world. We might leave the ordinary world through spirit flight or embrace our own godlike nature and reweave the threads of fate in spellcraft. All of these practices rely on our ability to create successful ritual. Whether alone or in groups, scripted or spontaneous, with minimalist or maximalist tastes, ritual is essential to what we do.

Not only is it what we do, but also ritual itself is by definition a matter of doing. *Ritual is a set of actions with symbolic value.* In this case, speech is an action and acts can be internal (visualization or saying words in the mind rather than aloud) and external. A symbol is an action, idea, or object that represents something greater or more abstract than itself. Symbols are important ways for all humans to express and create meaning, both within and outside ritual.

You're likely familiar with the types of rituals that witches do—including divination, communing with spirits, ritual possession, hedgeriding, celebrating seasons, spellwork, blessings. Although many witches share these broad types of ritual working, most of the rituals we enact have not been taken verbatim from a book or passed on orally in their full form through generations of practitioners. It is true that traditions may share elements of ritual and a witch will often borrow from older folk magic, but, even when we are working from folkloric source material or the published rituals of a fellow witch, we adapt things to our own needs. We deploy our intuition and the guidance of our spirit allies. It is beautiful to connect with what has come before and to read widely, but ultimately witches are often called on to do the creative work of transforming those sources into something novel, practical, and specific.

This sets our ritual apart from rituals that are broadly embraced in a society. Mainstream ritual practices typically have a tremendous weight of cultural sanctioning, hierarchical authority, and the comfort of relatively strict tradition. Participants are able to find considerable meaning through the repetition of the action and through the communal affirmation of the significance of the ritual. But we witches walk a peculiar path. Instead of relying on widespread social norms, our rituals often derive meaning from their ability to transform us into our most powerful selves and see truths that are obscured by the ordinary.

As many of us work solitary, we are often the only embodied, human performer and the only embodied, human audience. So ritual cannot be working only because we believe in the hierarchical power of somebody else, or because we value the approval and recognition of society, but rather because it necessitates a belief in ourselves as powerful. In itself this belief is revolutionary and transformative to many a witch. Because of the relatively egalitarian and participatory nature of most witchy groups, even group rituals work this way as each witch is an active participant and each is expected to give and receive.

Some witches feel put off by the theatricality of ritual. I used to be one of those witches, but I am now mostly cured. While some readers may have unsatisfying experiences, others may have wonderful experiences. If you have had ritual experiences in a group that felt fake or shallow, it's likely that some other participants experienced the same set of actions as profound and meaningful. It is typical for different folks to experience the same ritual differently, especially in larger, less intimately bonded groups. If past experience has caused the notion of ritual to lose some of its glamour, working on ritual by yourself can be a great way to experiment with what works for you, personally.

The word performative, which I have used to describe ritual, is often used in two different but related ways, both of which pertain to ritual. It is used to mean theatrical, sometimes with a negative connotation along the lines of being for show or "just a mask." But even in this negative context, aren't masks excellent aids in ritual? The obscured becomes clear and the costume becomes the real in successful ritual. Performative can also refer to words that do something rather than just describe something. For example, saying, "I dub thee, Sir Lancelot" makes Lancelot a knight and is not simply describing him as a knight. Most of our ritual is performative in both the sense of theatrical and, when it works, in the sense that it does something. Ritual may often be symbolic, but symbols participate in creating reality.

One fundamental thing that ritual does for witches is to alter our state of consciousness. The Hedgeriding chapter covers more of the nature and use of altered states, but apart from accidental occurrences like daydreams and spontaneous visions, much of what we do as witches uses ritual to create the altered states we work with. Like the states themselves, the functional ritual can vary from light and daily to intense and occasional. If your current practice involves a small, frequent ritual act like pouring water and saying a few words at an ancestor altar, that meaningful, ritual action slightly shifts your mental state; while a wild night of masked dance and ritual drama under the stars might shift your state more significantly.

Ritual can be a sticking point for many. If you are the lucky witch who has achieved a moment of utter contentment with the rituals of your life and craft, congratulations. You've done good work to get there. As an ever-growing Crafter, you will likely find yourself wanting to explore something new, push farther, or experiment. For the rest of us—ready for expansion, eager to give ourselves a little shove—ritual experimentation is a great starting point.

A Basic Ritual Outline

When confronted with the prospect of ritual creation, it can help to draw an analogy to various art forms. Those who are most skilled in choreography, musical composition, or a visual art may be able to connect stages of ritual to the stages of a creation in these arts. But the art and understanding of story is common across humanity, and most of us learned a simple structure of stories in school. When teaching children the elements of a story, we often start with the idea of beginning, middle, and end. Quickly we expand this to include the idea of climax and resolution. While there are no rules to ritual creation, below is a functional general structure based on the structure of narrative. For those who emphasize simple, spontaneous, and solitary ritual, you might not need to consider much in the way of structure or other tools of planned ritual creation. It may be enough to work intuitively, especially since narrative, or story, is such a part of human culture that we can hardly avoid it even when we're not working with it intentionally.

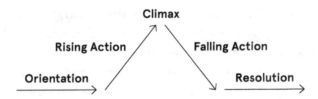

Orientation (Invitation and Intention)

Traditional narrative structure establishes who, what, where, and when, while rituals (especially with multiple participants) typically start by making clear the purpose of the ritual and asking allied spirits to participate. Either way the goal is to become oriented and immersed in the world of the story or ritual. The language used to state intent can range from the perfectly simple to the archaically ornate. If you are doing a solitary ritual, it may be enough to hold the purpose of the ritual clearly in your heart and mind as you begin. The beginning of the ritual is also when you can explicitly call on whichever spirits you will connect with. We make this call at the beginning of group rituals within my tradition, however oftentimes various beings are understood as always present; so just as much as we are inviting the spirits to attend to the ritual, we are also calling ourselves to a greater awareness of their presence, while focusing on the strength and immediacy of our connection to the various spirits we call.

Rising Action (Altered State Techniques)

Once you have made it clear what your ritual is meant to accomplish, it is time to set about accomplishing it. Rising action builds reader investment and suspense. Commonly, witches speak of raising energy during this phase, and if you are familiar with that concept it certainly applies here. Often the idea of raising energy is applied to directing raised energy for casting spells. That's fine, as spells are a kind of ritual. Not all rituals, however, are spells. In my own practice most are not. If the language of manipulating energy is the most resonant for you, just remember that you are still raising and directing energy, even if no other humans are involved.

Keep in mind that even if you are working as a solitary human, you are never working alone. You are working with the spirits and energies present in and around your location, your ancestors, your tools, any herbs or garb, and any deities you might work with regularly. These are your allies in this work, and each is like a coven member, with its own specific ways of being and working. You are the conductor, encouraging everyone in a harmoniously shared direction.

This stage can also be thought of as the buildup, building toward the climax, peak intensity, and the goal of your ritual. The exact techniques to use here are discussed more thoroughly elsewhere, but they range from a simple, muttered prayer to ecstatic dance. From a moment of focused meditation to elaborately guised ritual drama. Either way, when the tension cannot be held any longer or when you feel a quiet, intuitive *click* of rightness, it is time to shift to the next stage. Sometimes this transition is clear-cut and sometimes it is too gradual to precisely pinpoint.

Climax (The Central Working)

As the tension begins to reach its peak and participants are fully immersed in the work, the ritual transitions to the climax stage. This could look like hedgeriding, deep ritual possession, or the most powerful moment of ritual drama when reality twists into the shape of the performance. In quieter spirit work, it may be the moment of feeling a spirit's presence, receiving a message, or simply acknowledgement. Usually, the climax of a ritual will be easy to spot, because it will be a moment of excitement or quiet fulfillment and a release of energy. The moment of directing energy in most spellcraft marks the liminal transition between the climax and the falling action.

Falling Action (Return to the Ordinary)

This stage is usually much briefer than rising action. It's the gradual tapering off of the purpose of the ritual and the return to ordinary awareness. Depending on the nature of the ritual, this may be an intentional and planned return—back from the Otherworld or ritual possession. Other times, it is a subtle taper until participants are ready to close the ritual.

Resolution (Closing and Grounding)

Once you have done what you came to do, it is appropriate to ground excess energy, thank the spirits for their participation, ask for blessings, offer blessings, come back from a meditative or altered state, and generally wrap things up. Though you may choose to write a few special words to mark the completion of your ritual, the simplest form of this part of a ritual is some variation on the common phrase, "It is done."

On Sacred Space and Opening/Closing

All space is sacred, what changes is the practitioner's mindset. Your task in beginning a ritual is to create for yourself and other human participants a liminal consciousness, a betwixt and between place of the mind. You are beginning the process of lifting the foot that rests on the ordinary side of the hedge, and shifting your weight toward the foot that rests in the extraordinary unknown. If a sense of protection is needed for the work, that is typically created by inviting tutelary spirits who have an established and helpful relationship with the witch or witches.

Delineating the physical space that will contain the ritual can help with the shift in consciousness and there is a long history of that space being in the shape of a circle. Formally delineating the space matters little in quick, spontaneous, solitary ritual with tutelary spirits who just move with the witch to watch over the work. It can matter more as complexity, intensity, and number of participants rise. There are certain times that giving firmer boundaries to the ritual area can truly matter, such as when the goal of the ritual is to bring the entire circle with all participants into the Otherworld, or in intense ritual possessions that might need to be contained. Sometimes physical characteristics mark the boundaries (between the hickory tree and that boulder, for example); in that case, working with those boundary spirits can be helpful and appropriate to build a sort of memory of the space. If you desire to mark out a space, options include using yarn or another material for physical marking (but please don't sprinkle salt outdoors because it harms plants and the soil ecosystem). There are also many variations on pacing the outline, with or without words or song to accompany the movement, such as walking the outline while sweeping outward with a broom or tapping the boundaries with a staff or distaff. However, in a familiar location with a cohesive group, the boundaries of the space become so firmly entrenched in each mind that little outward marking is needed.

When circling with a new-to-you group or individual, it is wise to discuss how that person or group regards ritual space. What I describe here is true for my tradition and for many who have a more traditional bent to their practices. The end of this chapter includes a ritual opening and closing used by Forest's Edge members as an example that you are invited or use or modify. However, in the broader magical community, you are likely to find heavier Ceremonial or Eclectic Wiccan influence with a calling of guardians of watchtowers in each cardinal direction to help create an energetic bubble to protect and enclose a sphere of space set apart for sacred use.

On Tradition

I encourage all witches to design ritual elements that resonate for them and appropriately honor the spirits and beings with whom they work. Neither current trends nor my personal tastes need to be yours. At the same time, using ritual elements in common with other witches can build a sense of community and togetherness even when apart. When practicing in a group, it establishes a familiar rhythm and gets all participants aligned with the work. Whether you share elements with a local group of friends, like-minded souls separated by geography, or a tight-knit coven, you are creating a little piece of new tradition. Another way to establish community and continuity is through repeated elements of your own inventions or older bits of folk practice that can create links through time with your own group and with those magic practitioners who have gone before.

In the Forest's Edge tradition, we encourage diversity, and also share some features and philosophies regarding ritual in common:

- We keep a physical representation of our connection to the spirit of the tradition in our ritual space and honor that connection in ritual. For some this is an artistic work created intentionally to honor this spirit, and for others it is a different sort of object.

- We also honor ancestors, nature spirits, and often deities in ritual.

- We have an understanding that there is no unsacred space and regard ritual space primarily as liminal space and liminal consciousness, betwixt and between the worlds. Because most of the time the openings and closings of Forest's Edge rituals are geared toward building a sense of sacred liminality rather than of creating a protective bubble, social norms like treating the circle as an impenetrable boundary do not always apply. When a participant needs to leave the circle, if they can find the way back to the liminal space, then that participant is welcome to return.

- Because of this belief, it is more common for us to perform spiritual cleansing of ritual participants than to cleanse the ritual space, especially out-of-doors. Most of the time our circles are geared toward sacred liminality rather than protection.

- We perform certain rite-of-passage rituals tradition-wide.

Creating a Solitary Rhythm

For the traditional witch the goal is real, functional witchery. This means that it is essential for us to *do* our craft on a day-by-day, season-by-season basis. For some this is easy and obvious, while for others it is hard. These challenges can be long term or last only a season. One challenge can be that many of us are solitary witches. At the Forest's Edge, we say we are all solitary-in-community. This means that whether we have a local circle or not, we all cultivate solitary practice and work to maintain our ties to our tradition community. For a traditional witch with neither tradition nor local group, solitary-only practice can either be a sparkling gem of independence and self-direction or a quagmire of low motivation and prioritization. For many it is something in between. It can be hard to make practice a high priority if no one is waiting for you to light the ritual fire, but people are waiting for you to cook dinner. It can be especially hard for newcomers to believe in the reality of their work when there is no one to verify and celebrate with. Investing in your practices of divination, hedgeriding, spirit work, and spell casting, for your own sake, can be a part of spiritual growth.

Observing holidays that reflect the cycles of nature is an important part of being a witch and living into nature's rhythms. Observing these special days connects you to other witches and your spiritual ancestry and gives you a regular opportunity to tend to your spiritual needs. Having a sense of rhythm and connection that is integral to your life comes through your personal practices to a significant degree. The chapter Green and Local Witchcraft further explores the importance of seasonal and personal holidays.

If celebrating holidays or doing regular magical work does not always come easily to you, that is okay. We all have periods where practice lies fallow. We are all working to strengthen our spiritual practice and that process never ends. Start small by adding one new idea or practice at a time and find what works for you bit by bit. There is no hurry and no such thing as being finished. The following ideas are suggestions that have helped some witches through seasons of challenge.

1) Organize

If you do not already, it can be a good idea to put expected ritual dates into your calendar or planner. You might include full and dark moons, as well as any seasonal holidays you choose. If a doctor's visit deserves calendaring, then so too should your appointment with the spirits. You may even want to commit to setting a reminder for yourself a week prior to each event, so that you have some time to plan. Of course, this only works for cyclical observances, while much of your practice will be a response to emergent needs, intuition, and circumstances.

2) Find an Accountability Partner

A witchy accountability partner helps you stay accountable to your goals for practice, not through judgment but through interest and support. As social animals it means a lot to us when we share a plan with another person, who will then check in with us. It's a little bit of extra motivation. Teachers and mentors are typically one-sided accountability partners, where they check in on your practice but less fully vice versa. A fellow witchy friend (in person or online) can be a mutual partner, where you each check in equally and show interest in each other's process. If you have family or close friends who are witchy or supportive of your spiritual path, or both, you may want to ask one of those people to check in with you as well.

3) Create Default Rituals

Sometimes doing the same thing over and over feels like being stuck in a rut; but in terms of ritual, far more often it feels like having a consistent, dependable, spiritual practice—a tradition of your own with or without a larger tradition. So, start your own traditions! And then adjust them as needed. No one is going to make you stick with them always; you are entirely free to shake things up. However, the traditions you establish will be there for you when you need and want them.

Traditions can be just about anything that resonates for you. Maybe you want to make an offering at the base of your favorite tree on full moons, do some kind of house blessing each Autumn Equinox, or make a special dish each Winter Solstice and share it with your loved ones every year. Whatever works!

One great and foundational tradition is to create your own consistent ritual opening and closing and memorize it. Some witches begin and end ritual in very simple and intuitive ways most of the time, and reserve more formal ritual styles for special occasions. Just experiment until you find something that feels right to you.

4) Set a Yearly or Quarterly Theme

Setting a new theme for each year or seasonal quarter may sound limiting, but it is the kind of limit that can foster creativity, much like the limiting structure of formal poetry actually allows creative writing to blossom. It can seem counterintuitive, but having guidelines can really help us flourish. An example of a theme might be "Home and Hearth," "The Darker Mysteries," or "Nurturing Creativity," or it could be a focus on a certain deity or type of spirit. Let's say that "Home and Hearth" is your theme for this season. You might choose to do rituals that involve a house blessing, connecting with the spirits of your land, or working with a deity that signifies home and hearth. Another way of looking at a theme is to consider it as a goal but a more specific and inspiring goal than "practice regularly."

When setting a theme, try to choose something that is relevant to *you* at *this* specific moment in your life, rather than settling for a theme that is simply the stereotype of the season. What matters the most to you? What makes you the most excited? What do you need the most right now?

5) Experiment

No one is depending on you to create a spectacular ritual that meets *their* spiritual needs. The only person you have to satisfy is yourself. So, adopt a state of mind that invites play and creative ideas. If something sounds really new or too much or too hard, you should do it. Really! What is failure as a solitary? Even if things do not go as you had planned, you learned something. Experiment with your own adaptations of the ideas in this book as well. If you do not know whether a certain idea will work for you, try it. If it doesn't feel right, toss it.

6) Just Do It

If you feel tired, uninspired, overworked, bored, anxious, or what-have-you: *Do something anyway.* You do not have to feel in the mood to do a ritual. Coveners sometimes start a meeting by dragging themselves tired and stressed to another covener's house. They feel overwhelmed by their work, school, or family responsibilities and *even still* they spend hours at each coven gathering. Why? Because spending time on your spiritual practice is worth it. For many of us, our spiritual practice is what gives us extra strength to do other things in our lives—and to do those things well and from a place of soul-deep rootedness. Solitary, your rituals are likely to range from five minutes to an hour. Invest that much in yourself.

If you are feeling stressed or otherwise bad-vibe-y when you are trying to begin a ritual or other spiritual practice, try using a method of cleansing that works for you. One of the most common is to light a stick of herbs (homemade or store-bought) and gently waft the smoke over your whole body while your awareness begins to shift toward the magical. Just make sure the herbs are gathered ethically. A spritz with an essential oil spray can do a similar job. As can sweeping around yourself or your indoor altar with a broom or purpose-made feather duster. Or try something else that works for you: a few minutes of meditation or chanting, a bath, or a venting session with your sweetie.

Your observances may or may not look like what you imagine, but establishing a consistent practice is far more important than figuring out the perfect thing to do. There is no perfect. But there is such thing as a satisfying spiritual practice that is an authentic reflection of where you are *right now*.

The Creative Process of Ritual Writing

The first step in creating a ritual is determining why you need a ritual. Typically, you know you need a ritual when you have something important happening in which you want to involve the spirit world. Not all rituals need to be written down, and certainly not all rituals need to be long and complicated. Often, the most effective rituals are simple, short, and personal. However, whether they are simple or complex, the best rituals have a crystal-clear purpose, and every action performed in the ritual should tie back into the ritual's central focus for it to be truly effective.

Common reasons for having a ritual include:

- Celebration of holidays

- Consecration of an object

- Healing (including mental, physical, relational, self, others, land)

- Banishing something

- Beginning something

- Celebration of a life passage, such as birth, menarche, initiation, marriage, or death

- Hedgecrossing

- Sundry spellwork

- Seeking guidance

- Divination

- Addressing parts of one's own personality or experience

- Honoring a particular deity or other entity

Once you've decided on the central purpose or theme for your ritual, you may be wondering how to go about constructing it. The Practical Use of Magical Theory chapter may help guide your choices. A great way to get a sense of what rituals can and often do include is to attend rituals (be they religious or secular) and pay attention. If you have not yet had an opportunity to observe many rituals in person, try reading several different examples of rituals in books about witchcraft and Paganism. Keep the narrative structure of ritual in mind.

If you have a sense of how your ritual should flow, but you need inspiration for the lines participants will say, or if your ritual is for a holiday or in honor of a deity that you would like to know more about, it's always a good idea to do some research. The Internet and Pagan books can be a good place to start, but reading historical texts, such as poems written to a deity or historical accounts of how a holiday was traditionally celebrated, can also provide a great deal of material and inspiration. Writing rituals is a way to bring your creativity and intuition into play, but incorporating historical elements is also a wonderful way to feel connected to a larger community and deeper history.

If you are in the midst of writing a ritual and have already determined which elements you want to include but are at a loss for just the right words to use, do not despair! We all have the capacity to create beautiful rituals. However, each of us will do that in different ways. Some witches have a taste for verbosity, with flowery, arcane-sounding language. Some have a taste for direct language, pared down to emphasize powerful imagery and authenticity. Some draw heavily on language straight from folklore. Some prefer few words, if any, and instead emphasize symbolic, ritual actions. These are all equally skilled, creative, and magical ways to work.

Here are a few examples of ritual writing methods that you may want to try:

- Asking for inspiration in a dream or using a divination tool and interpreting the outcome

- Breaking the ritual down into components and writing them one at a time, then going back and working them all together to form a cohesive ritual

- Centering yourself, focusing on the intent of the ritual, and drawing whatever comes to mind and interpreting it

- Doing a walk-through of the ritual on your own, making notes about what worked and what didn't, and then sitting down to write the result of your trial-and-error experiment

- Making an outline of the basic ritual structure, incorporating your notes about your focus and any other elements into that outline, and then fleshing it out in one or more sittings

- Meditating, researching, and daydreaming, then sitting down and writing the whole thing in one sitting

- Turning the ritual creation process into a ritual itself, complete with opening and closing elements, where the meat of the ritual is seeking a flash of inspiration, a key image, or guidance from spirit allies

- Working with a partner or small group to gather ideas and to incorporate them into a ritual format

A Few Common Tools

For those unfamiliar with ritual tools, any introductory book on witchcraft can offer insight into the instruments commonly used by many modern witches. I encourage you to work with tools that speak to you. It is important to remember that they don't need to be fancy or expensive. Witches at the Forest's Edge typically prefer tools that are simple, natural, ethically sourced, and handmade. Most tools can be found in the average household or outdoors, or can be purchased second hand at thrift stores, flea markets, and even restaurant supply warehouses. It is never a requirement to purchase anything expensive or new, so do not let the lack of a specific tool stop you from doing the work of witchery. If you do want to make a special purchase, it is fruitful to consider the origin of the item. A tool handmade by a skilled artisan can have different spirit to it than a mass-produced item.

Keep in mind when reading about typical witch's tools that, as animists, we regard each tool as having a spirit. While *tool* is the simplest language we have for all the physical bits and bobs that we work with regularly in our Craft, we can also consider them working partners or allies. Each should be cleaned, cared for, thanked, and fed as it requires. A tool should be physically cleaned as appropriate to the material (for example, don't soak metal in water) and kept in good working order. This is a way of showing respect for the work that it does. Tools can be spiritually cleansed and blessed just like a human—including smoke, an essential oil spray, exposure to sunlight or moonlight, or herb-infused water. The spirit of the tool is fed by this care and many can benefit from additional feeding with an herb-infused oil. What follows are explanations of some of the tools currently central to my practice, offered as inspiration.

Altar: The witch's altar is a fundamental tool. Most of us have several, and we are also inclined to create little altars and shrines wherever we roam. An altar is any relatively flat space that you have set apart as being an altar for doing the work of witchcraft. It can be permanent or temporary. I've had shelves, desktops, fireplace hearths, tree stumps, and flatish stones serve as altars. I have built an outdoor altar of a large, flat stone atop smaller stones and an indoor altar of cabinet parts and reclaimed lumber. Whether tucked into a make-do nook or purpose-built, any altar is fine. In the event of a small shelf-type altar, you may find that much of your practical work is done in the kitchen or on the ground, either of which is also perfectly serviceable. Because many of us cook and process plants for magical herbalism only indoors, kitchen counters and the stove can become very altar-esque. *Some altars may have inherent tree or hearth symbolism, with roots or the hearth-stone connecting to the earth, and branches or a chimney reaching above, speaking to the flights that witches take to travel among the Otherworlds.*

Bell: I like this for opening and closing brief, low-key med-itations, especially with my kids. Mine is a vintage glass bell that creates a quiet, clear sound that seems to help my little ones (and me) enter into the right state of mind without any time-consuming pomp and circumstance. At times I have used a bell branch, which is simply a branch or wand with a number of small bells attached, but find that to be more of a calling or cleansing tool than a focus-inducing tool.

Blade: Although some choose a double-edged ritual blade, mine is a single-edged, handmade, Norwegian utility knife. The handle is carved from curly birchwood, the blade is triple-laminated steel, and the sheath is leather in a traditional Norwegian design. The single edge represents the interrelat-edness of all things and a single-minded focus on the work at hand. I also find single-edged blades more practical. I keep it sharp and in good condition, as the blade is used for physically cutting and carving materials as well as for energetic or sym-bolic cutting. Carefully cleaning, oiling, and sharpening the blade is part of what keeps it such a powerful tool. It is also handy for directing energy when a large staff is cumbersome or when the knife's pointy nature is symbolically appropriate.

Broom: Mine is handmade by me and used primarily for spiritual cleansing and also physical cleaning indoors.

Cauldron: Usually this is a mid-sized, antique cast-iron cauldron in my case, but sometimes my firepit is a sort of cauldron during outdoor rituals. I use cauldrons for blending ingredients, burning things, and occasionally for scrying. For edible things, I use a different cast-iron Dutch oven. Even a bathtub can be a cauldron that allows you to step into the potion.

Cup: This is not a single object but a type of object that is present in my rituals. There is a glass or cup of wine, mead, herbal tea, or some other beverage that I use to toast spirits and also to pour out offerings. I may make deity offerings, but more commonly the core of my offerings is for land spirits and ancestors. During indoor ritual certain ancestors of mine enjoy fresh spring water in a delicate teacup.

Rattle: My favorite rattle is homemade from a dried, garden-grown gourd, a shed antler, and natural pigments made from the stones in my creek. It is decorated with a symbol that signifies the magical dimension of my land. The general idea behind a rattle or drum is to have a very simple percussion instrument. Banging sticks together would suffice. A hollow log and a hickory knot can make a nice sound. The percussion instrument is used to induce trance, focus intention, call spirits, and for other uses.

Skull and Antler: A (replica) human skull is a home for and a symbol of my ancestors. The large antler rests behind it, curving around the sides in a crown-like way, combining a symbol for the spirit of the Forest's Edge and a particular local land spirit with human ancestry. Another variation I use particularly during winter months is of the human skull with a full rack of reindeer antlers set behind it. Some variation of antlers paired with a human skull has long worked very well for me, linking human, other-than-human, and tradition spirits, weaving together multiple layers of meaning. It also calls to mind the antlered human figures found across several cultures and time periods.

Staff: This is one of my most beloved tools. It's simply a large stick between shoulder and head-height. I have a few different staffs, from driftwood to hand carved to fresh from my forest. In many cultures, the staff has been among the central tools and status-markers of witches and shamans. I use my staff to mark out space and direct energy outdoors. I even tap it on the ground as something of a percussion instrument. The staff is frequently present in my ritual area because it symbolizes the world tree in addition to its other uses. Like a living tree, it is a physical representation of the link between the multiple worlds accessible to the witch.

Sometimes I work with a distaff, which is a staff with two or three prongs at the top. Cut from a small, forked tree, it serves the same practical uses and symbolism as the staff, with the added dimension that the distaff is a tool for wrapping and holding fiber when spinning. Weaving and spinning are a powerful metaphors for the way we work magic and, among other possible symbolism, the use of the distaff connects me to the work of the women of my ancestry and the witches of earlier times.

Veil: I use a large silk veil for ritual dance, ritual costuming and masking, and for mild sensory deprivation during hedge-crossing and ritual possession. Being draped or wrapped in the veil can create varying degrees of sensory deprivation. It is silk because silk is a natural fiber that is breathable and warm, yet so light that it floats magically when dancing. It is also relatively easy to dye silk, adding another opportunity for imbuing it with intent. I have dyed two in different colors, so I can choose the color best aligned with my work.

Other bits and bobs that function as ritual tools: Candles, mortar and pestle, my bag of bones and stones for divination and their wool casting cloth, tarot cards, various sorts of incense or smoke cleansing bundles, and any special ingredients I am using in a spell or other working. Various nature spirits are typically represented by the gifts of the land, from flowers to stones to bones.

A Ritual Opening and Closing Example

The altar is set up as host or participants choose, fire is built, and candles are lit. On the altar, the Forest's Edge tradition is generally represented by antlers, while ancestors are represented by a human skull. Land spirits are typically honored with something very local and any deities are represented as appropriate. The tokens on the altar are both symbolic representations and welcoming homes for the spirits.

All participants line up at the entrance to the ritual space. A sweeper sweeps in front of each person as they enter, to sweep away preoccupations and blocks to doing the work.

Spirits—tradition egregore, land spirits, ancestors and deities, or other spirits as appropriate—are invited with a spontaneous toast using language relevant to the work at hand. Each spirit ally or category of spirits can be invited by a different participant. If the ritual is on someone's private land, that person usually toasts the land spirits because they have the strongest working relationship there. The language used makes it clear that we are honored by the ever-present land spirits' permission to work in this place and that we invite them to lend a hand. Indeed, it is often acknowledged that many of these spirits are always with us. The overall essence of these toasts is of honoring, welcome, and a request for aid in the substance of the ritual. The toasts include an offering of the beverage being used.

The meeting's host thumps their staff or distaff on the ground three times. The visualization is of raising a hedge that symbolizes the liminality of shifting the space off kilter, into a wild, in-between space rather than of creating a protective bubble. We are crossing over into an Otherworldly consciousness.

All gradually raise their arms and chant:
Encircle now the compass round
Raise the hedge from sacred ground.
Where land meets sky and sky meets sea
Where blue meets grey and grey meets green

We lay this space betwixt and between.
All say: Our rite is begun.

The work of the ritual is conducted. Having food on hand is optional for grounding, although closing the ritual and then going elsewhere to eat is usually most convenient.

After the ritual, the spirits are toasted in gratitude in reverse order. Again, the language is spontaneous and particular to what has taken place. It hopefully goes without saying that spirit allies are not *dismissed* but rather thanked.

With the staff or distaff, the host taps the ground, slowly, three times. All raise and then gradually lower their arms, visualizing the hedge fading and the circle shifting back into ordinary space.

All say: Our rite is done.

Reflection

1. Is there something you've heard of other people doing that piques your interest?

2. Is there something that scares you a little? Maybe you're afraid you're unqualified to try something so serious? Maybe it's something you think a different kind of witch would do? Maybe it could be embarrassing or silly?

3. Have you been telling yourself you need something you don't currently have (a teacher, a coven, a garden, a tool) to try the new thing? We all have very real barriers to practice, but are you sure there's truly no way to make do?

4. Following the currents of your spiritual ancestry, how could your ancestors shape or expand your ritual practice? All cultures have ritual practices, from prayers for putting a hearth fire to bed to working a rosary to community-wide seasonal festivals and entheogenic practices (using substances to create spiritual, altered states); there's likely to be something fruitful.

5. Are there materials, attire, sounds, smells, locations, or other things that appeal to you? The sensory nature of ritual is such that it presents an opportunity to root ourselves in the physical body and all of its senses. What do your senses crave?

6. What is beautiful? What is powerfully, meaningfully, beautiful to you might be scary, ugly, silly, or strange to an outsider, or it might align nicely with societal notions of prettiness. Either is equally valid.

7. Have you had wonderful ritual experiences? Crappy ones? Was there one thing that worked in an otherwise mediocre ritual experience? Reflecting on what has made the good *good* and the bad *bad* might offer some direction.

8. For those of us with long experience working with groups, do you carry any difficult emotions left over from past experience that could impact your opinion or experience of ritual? I know I'm not the only one who does, or the only one who has found some freedom in sorting through that.

Practice

- Create a solitary ritual opening and closing. If you already have one in use, have you found ways it could be refined? Even if you are perfectly happy with what you have, it can help to try something new as well. If it is currently simple, try experimenting with complexity. If it is verbose, try a less wordy, more active method. If it is spontaneous, try a bit of planning.

- Create a ritual to share with others. This could mean a ritual to be performed with a group or to be done by multiple people, separately. Jot down any feedback you receive.

- If you have any specific weaknesses or challenges in planning and executing ritual, dig straight into those. If you are uncomfortable with ritual movement or dance, try it. If you think you're not good at writing inspiring ritual words, do it.

7

HEDGERIDING

When the witch's spirit lets loose of the body and flies into other realms, it is real, thrilling, powerful. And sometimes, it is dangerous. Many witches conduct their craft without ever doing such a wonderfully absurd thing. Many do not feel called to this practice and are excellent, effective witches, nonetheless. But for traditional witches, the ability to cross over into the Otherworld and work with spirits of various ilk is vital. Indeed, folkloric depictions of witches are rarely complete without a flying broom or some other reference to flight.

Hedgeriders follow in the ancient tradition of magical practitioners who live with one foot in this world and one foot in the Otherworld. The Otherworld is the multilayered realms of fae, ancestors, gods, and innumerable other spirits. Hedgeriding is a means to release part of our consciousness from this world and travel, spiritually, into the Otherworld to engage with spirits, gather new knowledge, hone magical skills, and create change. A skilled hedgerider fully lives out the liminal balance—and deep connection—between this world and other realms. Witches who use this technique can be called hedgewitches. Hedgeriding is just one possible term among several for this practice. Spirit flight is an equally apt one, and I use that language interchangeably.

It is one of the two skills an apprentice in my tradition must master before being considered fully fledged (pun intended) and ready to attempt the initiation ritual (the other skill being ritual possession, which creates a nice balance between sending your spirit *out* and inviting another spirit *in*). Like any skill, some will take to hedgeriding more readily, while others will find the practice more of a challenge. Neither is better or worse. The same goes for divination, spellcasting, and ritual possession. It's just a matter of inclination and difference, like learning math and reading. In the end, you almost certainly learned to do both with at least tolerable proficiency.

Why "Hedgeriding"?

In other religious and magical traditions with similar practices, what I call hedgeriding may also be known as shamanic journeying or by a variety of other terms. Many readers will be more familiar with the language of shamanism, which comes originally from the Tungusic-speaking people of Siberia. Many in the broader occult community became familiar with the idea as neo-shamanism, which tried to distill key elements across cultures to create a non-specific, non-religious set of ecstatic spiritual techniques. Unfortunately, white, non-Indigenous, and often male neo-shamanic practitioners generated controversy by appropriating religious knowledge from distinct and diverse Indigenous groups in the Americas to meet their own spiritual needs. This cultural appropriation conducted under the banner of shamanism somewhat tarnished the language of shamanism for modern witchcraft. The other trouble I find in using the language of shamanism is that its definition can vary from broad to narrow depending on the historian, practitioner, or anthropologist using it. Shamanism can simply be a way to induce spiritual ecstasy, or it can draw on a variety of characteristics that may not apply to modern, traditional witchcraft.

In contrast, hedgeriding and hedgewitchery are terms arising from modern witches, drawing on linguistic, historical, and folkloric influences from Europe. Because much of my own Craft draws on sources from Europe, this is reasonable match. Over time the Forest's Edge tradition has shifted from saying we practice shamanic witch-craft to using the language of hedgewitchery and hedgeriding once those terms became acknowledged in the community. That said, our practices haven't changed a bit, so it is a matter of semantics. Famil-iarity with the scholarship on shamanism will be invaluable to the modern hedgewitch as shamanism is the term used in English to describe the animistic practice of sending the spirit forth from the body for sundry purposes. The resources list at the end of this book offers some starting points.

Each culture that uses a related ecstatic spiritual technique has very specific rituals, materials, religions, and lore. As you dig into your spiritual ancestry and cultural roots, you may find language related to those cultures or traditions that you prefer. It is the doing of the thing that matters most. The language is a matter of personal preference.

Putting the Hedge in Hedgeriding

At a pasture's edge, a man chops partway into the trunk of a small tree, bending it to tuck it in neatly with a seemingly endless row of similar trees. Where each tree has been wounded, new growth sprouts and in this mutual construction of human and nature smaller plants find comfortable nooks. Within the interwoven network of green life, fungi and animals thrive. Swift-footed creatures race through this picturesque highway that links pockets of wilderness. This is a hedgerow and it is a far cry from the manicured monoculture of evergreen shrubs that folks plant around houses or apartment buildings and call a hedge.

The hedge in hedgeriding is likely better understood through an English farmer's hedgerow than an American's front yard. Both mark boundaries, but a traditional hedgerow is a collaboration between humans and diverse fellow creatures. A hedgerow harbors a complete ecosystem, is an important habitat, and can provide a variety of things that we humans need. Those with decorative hedges or a privacy screen of trees may not have the traditional hedgerow, but they can see the ancestral echo of one.

Where I live, we have neither a manicured hedge nor a traditional hedgerow. I live in a North American deciduous forest and where the forest meets meadow an ecological edge is created. There is a short, transitional space of shrubby, thorny, often edible species before unfettered forest rises from the earth. This transitional space that marks the boundary is my hedge. Trust that wherever you live, there are edges, the liminal spaces that call our spirits forth. Whether a British hedgerow, a suburban hedge, a roadside, or another ecological edge, this liminal space of the hedge speaks to the work of being a witch with one foot here and one foot in the Otherworld. The work of hedgeriding is to shift your awareness from one foot to the other at will. As witches, the hedge is a place that calls to us, but one that we must also respect. The traditional hedge is quite difficult to traverse. But if you wish to dip your toes into the churning waters of the Otherworld, a hedge is a good place to go.

To ride means to travel through and over, in or on something, or to be borne by. Married with the idea of the hedge, this means that the practitioner does not just pass through or over the boundary between this world and the next, but that they are also simultaneously borne by it, straddling those two worlds and riding the liminal. Expanding upon the image of the hedge and its richness, one might say that the practitioner is borne forth by the complex tangle of all that makes up their individual path—relationships with various spirits, ancestors, and deities; rituals and seasonal observances; and the knowledge of Otherworldly lore. The hedge is the boundary to be crossed but is also the journey itself. It is full of thorns but also full of life. A journey to the Otherworld can be difficult but also rich with reward. Thus, the hedge is itself the vehicle.

Axis Mundi—of Maps and Means

From the depths of the underworld to the peaks of the gods, with our world in between, the *axis mundi* is a map of the worlds and a means of connection among them. While the term astronomically refers to the vertical line that can be imagined as running through the center of the earth between its poles, mythologically speaking it is the vertical line that connects the realms of spirits to our own. It is one way of bringing order to the multilayered universe through a clear image. In different cultures, this idea may take different forms: a mountain, a pillar, a vine. Perhaps its most familiar incarnation is as a tree, the world tree.

Many who engage in some form of spirit flight describe where they are going and how they get there through the image of the world tree. Often the notion of the world tree separates the Otherworld into upper and lower realms to create a comprehensible categorization. Spirit flight is traveling up and down the trunk, roots, and branches of a great tree that connects the worlds. Typically travelling up to the branches is said to lead to the heavens or the upper world of gods and cosmic architecture. Travelling down to the roots, you reach the underworld, a place of the dead and spirit guides. This leaves the trunk of the tree as the middle world, where we live and fairies live—just a bit off-kilter from us. Several world cultures have a tree of this sort with specific narratives, names, and so forth. Depending on your individual sense of spiritual ancestry, this image may resonate for you in either general contours or through cultural specifics.

If the world tree or another axis mundi resonates with you, consider integrating it with your preparations for hedgeriding. Planning where you will be travelling on the axis is a way of solidifying your intentions for the work, and the sensations of moving upward or downward can be integrated into your preparatory visualizations as discussed below. Although it can be useful, it is important not to mistake the map for the terrain. There is nothing high about gods nor low about ancestors. They are not actually separate at all or necessarily in different places. I prefer to avoid the binary of high versus low, and instead view the axis mundi as simply as a network of connection among the multilayered worlds. It is not necessary to work with world tree imagery at all if it does not suit you.

Astral travel, or projection out of one's body in the middle world is a concept that is popular in New Age circles and often does not involve intentional work or engaging with with spirits. Hedgeriding can encompass this kind of practice or exclude it. Some who have a natural talent for this skill may find middle world travel to be the easiest gateway into hedgeriding, because it does involve the spirit leaving the body and being able to visit other people and locales within this more familiar reality. However, the hurdle of shifting into a fully other reality must still be jumped.

The idea of the axis mundi is also reflected in other vertical imagery that you may find in witchcraft. Another image that informs my hedgeriding is that of the hearth. Witches now and in the past sometimes practiced at their hearths, not only for the practicality of tools at hand but also because the hearth is a liminal space—the vertical chimney is a portal to the outside, and the hearth fire is the cooking fire, a place of creation, of alchemy. The hearth stone itself is a powerful connection to the underworld as well as to earthy power. The axis mundi is also represented by wells, staffs, brooms, or distaffs. Folklore tells of magical practitioners flying up their chimneys, often on broomsticks, to ride the winds and do their work in the world. All of these representations of the axis mundi serve as reminders of our nature as hedgewitches. We ride the hedge, we find the way, we cross boundaries, and we travel between the worlds.

Hedgeriding and Guided Meditation

At its core, hedgeriding is a deeply altered state of consciousness and both mental and physical. The witch is creating the state and choosing what to do with it in a general sense, but one way or another that shift in the state of consciousness past the point of control must occur. Sometimes this highly altered state is called religious ecstasy or a kind of trance state. Whatever the language, your normal way of sensing, perceiving, and being *changes*. The good news is that everyone's state of consciousness changes every day—from waking to sleeping, from distraction to focus, from daydream to present mindedness. And while the most ecstatic states may be rarer—within sexual acts, collective dancing, deep creative engagement, and moments of glory in nature—they too are quite normal for humans. An adequately altered state requires a flow, a release of control. We *must* let go. And yet, hedgeriding witches take this normal human capacity and practice until we know how to induce the state, use it, and end it at will. It is something of a paradox. But then paradox, too, is the birthright of humanity.

It is important to point out that guided meditation or pathworking is not hedgeriding. Visualization, spirit sensing, and imagination are incredibly useful tools, and they can open the door to hedgeriding, but the witch must cross into the Otherworld to actually experience hedgeriding. While using guided meditation, your own mind is creating imagery that you can experience inwardly. Perhaps you are directing the meditation or maybe you are listening to a recorded guide's voice. Either way, the events occurring are your creation. For some hedgeriders, their experience is similar to this—lushly visual, linear, and narrative in structure—with one important difference. At some point things begin to occur that the witch did not create, and at that point the hedgeriding has begun.

While it's true that guided meditation is not hedgeriding, it is often a solid place to start when learning to ride the hedge. Whether on your own or with a teacher or a group, developing a detailed and powerful visualization can help you take your first intentional steps into the Otherworld—increasing those skills by picturing what someone else is describing. The next step is to guide yourself in such visualizing, clearly seeing images of your own choosing. And although that kind of activity is often called visualization, it is really best done using all the senses.

If this method appeals to you, it can help to start by creating a hedgeriding waystation—a vividly imagined location. The location can be real in this world or utterly made-up. For some, a location within our reality can honor local land spirits and help anchor you to this world for your return journey. While for others, a place picked from the mythic landscape of your own mind can feel closer to the Otherworld in some sense. Get to know this place intimately, using all your spirit senses. While in this location, practice calling on the ancestors, nature spirits, or other allies you would work with while hedgeriding for guidance, protection, and other help.

Once you have mastered visiting your waystation, it is time to expand your spirit-sensing experience and see yourself leaving it in some way. By whatever portal you choose to leave your waystation, be it a doorway, a chimney, an archway of roses, a hollow log, or stepping over a stream, this leave taking is a symbolic step away from one reality and toward another. At this point, you are still in control of what you are seeing and otherwise experiencing. Eventually, with enough practice, this altered state of consciousness can become deep enough that you can easily cross over into the Otherworld. You will know you have made the crossing when the unexpected can happen. This shift can be subtle, and easily missed the first few times it happens. Occasionally it is difficult to discern whether you have slipped into the Otherworld, or merely fallen asleep and begun to dream during this process. You will learn to trust your intuition regarding these experiences, and adjust your practices accordingly. Keep in mind, the hedge is not just a one-way street. You will begin to see the places where the Otherworld crosses back to confirm your experiences or reach out to you in your own this-world spaces. That can be eerie at first, but it can also be powerfully affirming for you as you take your hedgeriding deeper.

A Mixed Bouquet of Methods

While visualization and meditation are a good starting place, they will not be equally effective for everyone. I have found that roughly three-quarters of witches do well beginning with visualization and guided meditation before sliding deeper into true hedgeriding. However, there are many ways a practitioner can achieve an altered state for hedgeriding. Below are some other methods, all of which should be approached with discernment and responsibility. These methods can be used in combination and successively to gradually deepen the altered state. This is not a medical text and it is wise to consult a physician regarding practices such as substance use and intensive physical activity.

- **Rhythmic practices** like drumming, dancing, pacing, and chanting can be extraordinarily powerful for most witches. These techniques can be a tonic for those who struggle with falling asleep during deep meditation or achieving deep states of meditation while sitting still. Some form of rhythm or percussion is a cornerstone of hedgecrossing technique for most practitioners. Whether bodily, vocal, or instrumental, finding the rhythm that calls your spirit into flight will likely be key. Other rhythms, beyond dance and percussion, are also effective, including rhythmic natural movements such as the flickering of flame or the rippling of water.

  Another less active form of rhythmic immersion is a focus on breath and control of the pattern of breathing. A controlled breathing technique or simple breath-awareness can be used before, during, after, or in place of a more active technique to amplify its effect.

  One good starting point is breathing around the cross-quarters. Think of a compass rose and the liminal spaces between North, South, East and West. Breathe into those spaces while counting to four. Breathe in for four counts (Northeast). Hold in for four counts. Breathe out for four counts (Southeast). Hold out for four counts. Breathe in for four counts (Southwest). Hold in for four counts. Breathe out for four counts (Northwest).

- **Substances** such as herbal flying ointments containing nightshades, burning herbs like wormwood and mugwort, herbal

The Witch at the Forest's Edge

ritual smokes, alcoholic beverages, and other substances can be employed by practitioners to assist in creating altered states. Some herbal substances are worked with predominantly for their magical properties or spirit alliances, while other have a direct physiological effect like any drug. Obviously, these substances all carry risks that vary from practitioner to practitioner, and I do not recommend employing any method that might damage a practitioner's health or result in other problems. It is absolutely *not* necessary to work with flying ointments or other active substances. But if the spirits of these plants and fungi call to you, pursue learning about entheogens. Begin sparingly and increase the dose as needed, being mindful of set and setting. Remember, while much is made of the aesthetic witchiness of these substances, in truth most hedgeriding is done without any of it.

- **Places of power** such as mushroom rings, natural springs, caves, cliffs, beaches, rings of stones, forest clearings, and of course actual hedges, can be sought out and partnered with to ride the hedge. Such places are liminal in and of themselves and in a sense working with this kind of physical location is helpful like any partnership or alliance. It is important to develop a relationship with such places, and any individual spirits that may dwell there, especially through the practice of offerings and asking what is needed. Tending to the physical care of a location you work with repeatedly can be a powerful step, whether the location is a back garden or the rare ecosystem of a cedar glade. And, of course, it is also important to ensure one's physical safety and privacy in such a place. Nonetheless, this way of working with physical locations can have an element of mild danger or at least uncertainty that for some really lends itself to the wild and mysterious nature of spirit flight.

- **Liminal spaces** are found not only in nature, but also within our daily living spaces as well. Standing in a doorway or an open gate, sitting at a hearth or by a crossroads, by a window or on a stairway landing, or even standing on one foot with one eye closed can put you in the in-between and familiarize you with the power of the liminal.

- **Sensory deprivation** is another technique with ancient roots. Most commonly, we now use this technique when we deprive our sight of enough light for clear (ordinary) sight or when we use a veil, shawl, or cloak to cover or wrap ourselves. Even some masks have an element of this in the way that they may partially obscure vision and cover the sensitive skin of the face. Finding a way to completely isolate oneself from sound is another option within this category. Sensory overload is a flip side to this technique, and the loud music and lights in settings like a dance club can work in this way.

- **Ritual and repetition** can include all of the above methods, but also emphasize physicality and habit. By repeating the same words and gestures time and again, crossing can become a habit that is more easily re-activated at will. Ritual elements (discussed at much greater length in the chapter Creating Ritual) can also act on the would-be hedge crosser in a variety of ways. Consider the objects (invited to work as spirit-filled allies), transformative ritual attire, cleansing, and preparatory practices that you choose as part of your hedgecrossing technique.

Experience, Depth, and Doubt

While some hedgeriders take to it like ducks to water and quickly become confident in their own experiences, others may struggle in various ways. Perhaps it is difficult to make the shift from consciously trying to create an altered state to relinquishing control. It is a strange and very witchy paradox that we use focus and control to let go and do something wild. Sometimes the struggle is shyness or negative comparison or fearfulness of trying it without a partner. Sometimes it comes of rational self-doubt and the lingering question of, "Is this real?" There are as many unique challenges as there are witches, but they can be overcome, eventually.

For me, I sometimes sense the transition to hedgeriding from an altered but this-world awareness as flying or falling through a dark but starlit sky. My sensory awareness of ordinary reality fades. When witches hedgeride, we say that *part* of our spirit flies. The spirit is not wholly separated from the body. We notice that when hedgeriding, a portion of our awareness can often, although not always, continue to sense ordinary reality. Simultaneously we may be deep in the Otherworld, while also slightly aware that our body is resting among autumn leaves beside the warmth of a fire. The degree to which this-world awareness remains is influenced by several factors: the preference and experience of the witch, the witch's sense of this-world safety, the purpose of the work, and the witch's role in a group that's working together. As a group leader, I often maintain some extra awareness to be able to return quickly in the event that a less-experienced group member needs support. When I am alone in the forest at night, I keep some light awareness for physical safety. The situations, reasons, and degree of gone-ness that each witch prefers and experiences is entirely individual, tied to both psychological and circumstantial specifics.

Ultimately, we choose for ourselves how much awareness remains. Newer practitioners may have less control over the degree of depth than more experienced witches. Some are more prone to leave very little, if any, awareness behind. Others' tendency is to fly lightly. Regardless of degree, it is all hedgeriding and it all counts. If you are desirous of deeper experience, reflection on those internal or external limiting factors may help you design a path toward a more fully *gone* experience.

On Health and Precautions

Hedgeriding is typically safe in the literal, physical sense. Although crossroads and train tracks have folkloric appeal, they are wisely avoided in this case. Your basic common sense for working in a relatively secure location with trustworthy people (or alone) is probably adequate for physical safety. Usually it does not present many more spiritual or psychological hazards than any other deep, inner work. Although some begin hedgecrossing with a combination of intrigue and trepidation, there's honestly no need to approach this practice with excess fear. This practice is ancient and deeply human. The serious pitfalls are more the exception than the rule. That said, it would be wrong of me to champion this practice and imply that there is no danger at all. Travelling in this world is not entirely safe or certain, but with those uncertainties come great rewards. So it is with Otherworldly journeying.

I do need to mention mental health, here. On one hand, spiritual practices, including hedgeriding, can play a very positive, transformative role in mental health and wellness. The altered state of consciousness created here can give the mind space to integrate feelings and experiences. The kind of healing won through spiritual practice can be gentle and soothing or incredibly intense and painful. Most hedgeriding related to personal, spiritual, or ancestral wellness falls within a spectrum of positive, if uncomfortable, growth.

One thing to look out for is when hedgeriding becomes an absorbing escape that dims the light of ordinary reality. Hedgeriding is not meant to diminish your enjoyment of or participation in everyday life. If it is commonly quite difficult to come back, that should also sound a note of concern. Repeated frightening interactions in Otherworlds is another a signal to pay attention. Working through deep ancestral traumas or engaging with tricky or harsh spirits is often part of a witch's practice *on purpose,* but if malicious interlopers keep cropping up *unexpectedly* despite the witch's efforts, that's a warning sign best heeded. Significant mental health conditions can occasionally complicate matters and if or when that happens, readers are encouraged to seek the support of a mental health professional as needed.

Given that hedgeriding usually goes just fine when it is achieved, there are just a few reasonable safeguards to consider.

- **Know your host:** If you are visiting a spirit on their own territory, much as you might go to a friend's house for tea, know whom you're seeking and keep in mind their temperament, companions, and ethical sensibility. As witches who form meaningful and mutual partnerships with various beings, it should go without saying that knowing the terrain of that relationship is powerful.

- **Have a way back:** It helps to know your way back to our world. What exactly that means can vary. If you have begun with a visualization, it could make sense to repeat it in reverse. If you have travelled through a landscape while hedgeriding, you may want to mark a trail or keep a mental map. Or you could have a phrase or chant pre-determined as something akin to a safe word to draw yourself back. Hedgeriding with a magical, physical object in your (this-world) hand is a powerful, tactile way to remind yourself of the return. The item's spiritual essence can fly with you, giving you a tool in the Otherworld. Some choose a key for this purpose, a cord to follow back, or a small pouch with several allied objects. Most experiences of hedgeriding tend to resolve themselves, with the practitioner realizing they have returned. Or the witch can simply decide to return and do it. As practice allows you to cross more easily and remain more fully in the Otherworld, an established way back is useful. It can also feel more secure to let go and fly wildly into other realms when there's a return-trip already planned.

- **Invite guardians and allies:** Human or otherwise, it is wise to have a partner invited to safeguard your body and light the way home. At times you may also want a guide in the Otherworld. For many, a human companion is undesirable or not possible, but one of the tutelary spirits with whom you regularly work can do just as well.

- **Pay attention to spirit sensing and intuition:** The skills you have developed in sensing and shielding yourself from undesirable energies in this reality will apply equally or even more so in the Otherworld. But keep in mind that generally the more control you exert over an experience, the less profound you allow it to become.

- **Bring a cutting tool:** Rarely needed, but occasionally useful, you may want to have a cutting tool with you, such as a ritual blade. Once in a while, depending on the sort of work you undertake, you may find yourself with a stowaway spirit trying to tag along with you back to our world. This is almost always to be discouraged and a ritual blade can be used to sever energetic ties to hangers-on.

Thirteen Steps from Here to There

Many years of teaching this practice has taught me that different approaches work best for different people. The imagery and ideas offered above are more than enough for some to either begin or further develop their practice. While others—including witches who do not typically work with other hedgeriders in person—find they need to begin or progress by seeing some more clear-cut steps laid out. If you have no trouble with hedgeriding, then this outline probably is not for you unless you are teaching an apprentice. These steps exist for those witches who find that structure and as much logic as possible fosters rather than hinders their access to the magical dimensions of life.

1. **Preparation:** First, know your reason. Why are you trying to ride the hedge? This will of course determine where, in the many realms of the worlds, you are aiming to go. Prep work also includes: Ensuring that you have spirits who will look out for you while you travel, forging a relationship with any specific entities you are planning to visit, and selecting and gathering materials for whatever form of altered state induction you choose. If you prefer to work from a familiar visualized space as a waystation, spend time in that space in advance until you know the feeling of that space intimately, like a key fitting into a lock.

2. **Invitation:** Set up your ritual space, make toasts or offerings, and call on any and all spirits you want to guide and guard you. For some witches, safe, familiar locations are best, while for others wild, slightly dangerous spaces better evoke the flying state. A space that is liminal itself is ideal. Do what you usually do to raise the hedge.

3. **Intention:** You already know inwardly your reason for crossing and now is the time to state it clearly and ask that all spirits present (including your own) help you work toward that goal. This could be a clear thought, a spontaneous statement, a carefully crafted poem, a chant, or some combination thereof.

4. **Centering:** While stating your intention, you begin to center yourself. To do this, you gather your wandering energy and your scattered awareness toward the center of your being, so that you become focused on the task at hand, present in the moment, and able to travel in accord with your will.

5. **Altered state induction:** This takes many different forms, as discussed above and in the Creating Ritual chapter.

6. **Letting go:** This often happens simultaneously with altered state induction. You have thrown yourself down the rabbit hole in pursuit of your goal, and at some point you will have to let go if you don't want to be snapped back into ordinary reality like a bungee jumper. You are releasing—or temporarily setting just a wee bit to the side—any self-protective snark, fear of losing control, self-criticism, and the voice of our society that probably echoes somewhere in your own mind that says, "This

is impossible," in order to reach out to and hold on to a powerful trust—in yourself, your tradition, and your spirit allies.

7. **Crossing:** In one form or another, you travel. It will be dependent on your method of altered state induction and your personal preferences and skills. Perhaps you are moving your physical body across a physical threshold. Perhaps in spirit you are aware of yourself running or flying in human or animal form. Perhaps you feel a moment of vertigo before your senses shift and expand. Perhaps you are using a planned visualization and suddenly you're not creating it anymore.

8. **Mystery:** You're here. Now go do what you set out to do.

9. **Return:** One way or another, you will be done. Mission accomplished or just tuckered out for the time being. If you use music or drumming to go, you can use the same thing to help on the return. If you use a waystation, go back there first before returning fully. The return crossing happens in reverse. Begin to feel your bodily senses again. Try focusing on each sense in turn.

10. **Centering (again):** You have just travelled a great distance and are now regaining an ordinary awareness of your own body and ordinary senses. Once again you are gathering yourself together, pulling your scattered energy into your core, and being present in the moment. Be gentle with yourself. Crossing is work, so take whatever time you need.

11. **Storytelling:** Either discuss your experience with others, record your voice, or jot down some notes—you are apt to start

forgetting details once you ground fully. Be sure to consider the emotions and intuitions attached to the events. If you have lingering questions, jot them down for future hedgeriding, divination, dream incubation, or research.

12. **Grounding:** Likely grounding (or returning to a balanced, stable connection with the earth and your body) will be a gradual process as you return. Be sure you are fully grounded and feeling relatively normal (but probably tired) before you go to bed. If you feel jittery or high or spacey, you have not grounded properly. Any grounding method is acceptable—including food and drink, bare feet, contact with the earth or with a hearthstone, or a grounding visualization.

13. **Gratitude:** Wrap up the ritual in whatever way you like and be sure to emphasize your gratitude to those who have been your guardians and guides. You can simply say "thank you," or add more poetry to it.

Into the Mystery

Proficiency at riding the hedge is an ongoing process for all witches who engage in the practice. Like most aspects of the Craft, it is a highly personal practice, developed through experience. It is also one of the aspects of practice known as a mystery, or something that must be experienced to be truly known. Like the practice of witchcraft itself, it is infinitely challenging and rewarding.

Reflection

1. What are your concerns and fears associated with riding the hedge? How can you confront these before attempting your first crossing, or can you?

2. Is there a cultural model that you resonate with when it comes to riding the hedge? Why does it resonate with you specifically, and can *you* use it? How does it differ from this model centered on the ideas of hedges and European witchcraft? How is it similar?

3. If you are relatively new to hedgeriding, what spirit allies will you work with to assist you? What tools would make you feel prepared and secure?

4. If you have an established hedgeriding practice, what methods do you use to induce an altered state of consciousness? Are there other methods you may find unsettling or intimidating, allowing you to push the edges to produce continued growth?

5. If you are a new hedgerider, what method or sequence of methods of inducing an altered state will you try first? If you are uncertain, consider what works for you in other aspects of life. Does dancing light you up and refresh you? Do you like to zone out to music? Are you a quiet daydreamer? Imaginative? A skilled meditator? Does getting dressed up and putting on makeup shift your mood and get you ready for the day?

Practice

- Practice a self-guided meditation that leads you to a waystation with several options for crossing over—perhaps there is a hedge, a cave, and a stone archway. Visit this place repeatedly and try each of these portals in turn without expectation for what you may find on the other side. When you come out of meditation, record your experiences. Finally, visit this place in your imagination without any preconceived notion of what portal you may find there, and see what happens.

- Select a more active or physical method of inducing trance and employ it, if you are currently accustomed only to meditative practices.

- Take walks and find places that feel like hedge spaces. Take notes. Make it a goal to explore and discover these places in your world on a regular basis.

- Record your dreams upon waking every night for a week. Then engage in a trance-inducing activity, and record your experiences. Compare and contrast the nature of these experiences as an exercise in building confidence and discernment.

8

DIVINATION

Divination is one of the most widespread and well-known practices of modern witchcraft, ancient religion, and magic. From Mesoamerica to Ancient Greece to the Bible, divination is a remarkably popular practice across human history. From noticing three birds against a twilight sky to scattering bones on a cloth, divination holds a special place in the hearts of witches. Unlike other skills that I stress in this particular form of traditional witchcraft, like hedgeriding and ritual possession, this one seems nearly universal.

Divination is a way to seek knowledge of the unknown. To be divination, it must be intentional and require interpretation of the results. With etymological roots connected to the divine or the sacred, divination is one way to interact with a god or, more broadly, a spirit. There are plenty of other ways that people interact with the spirits, including prayer, offerings, invocation, and worship, but divination has a distinction that many of these other methods do not: the spirits speak back immediately. Often, the diviner also has the benefit of physical divinatory objects showing the response, which can feel easier to believe than an intuitive sense with nothing that seems like verification.

Spirits of Inspiration

As a diviner making an intentional inquiry, who is "on the other side" of those cards, coins, sticks, or stones? For a traditional witch the possible answers are many. You may be asking your questions only of the spirits of the divinatory system itself. You may be asking gods, ancestors, or any other spirits. Or, it may be that the person you're really talking to is yourself. Using divinatory methods to commune with your subconscious or any other internal part of *you* is perfectly valid. Additionally, none of these divinatory sources are mutually exclusive. If you choose, you can use a divination system to communicate with a combination of sources to get answers that work on multiple levels.

The nature of being an animist doing divination is that you are not only learning a symbolic language, and not only forming a relationship with the spirits on the other side, but also you are working with the spirit of the divination tool itself. Although it can be much easier to perceive the spirits of a personal or natural divinatory collection of stones and bones, even a factory-made deck of tarot cards has its own spirit and spiritual ancestry, a history connected with the meanings encoded in their forebearer decks and centuries of interpretation. They also carry a bit of the intention imbued by their particular authors and artists, and the authors and artists who influenced them. They even have a bit of tree-spirit in their paper. A deck's individual spirit grows and develops through interaction with you, and experienced readers will tell you that each deck is oddly individual.

As you strive to honor the spirit of any divinatory system, you will find that the objects used for divination (of the casting lots type, see below) will require a special kind of care. Some are fed or empowered by oils, herbal washes, or blood; some are kept in a special container or cleansed in a certain way. When working within a specific system, it is important to pay attention to the traditional ways of treating and honoring the tools that you use. You may also find that the specific items you use prefer somewhat idiosyncratic care and feeding.

If you do not currently have a practice of caring for your divinatory tools, an intuitive starting place is to use the system to ask the system. Keep a lookout for responses that can be interpreted as asking for cleansing and blessing by smoke or fire, water (perhaps a water-based herbal spray), stones, or infused oils. You may notice a preference for location, such as, to be kept in darkness, to bask in sunlight or moonlight, or to be taken outdoors periodically. Whatever the means, the principle of treating divinatory materials with respect is an important part of forming a productive relationship with a given system.

Fortune Telling and Play

Different forms of divination have been used for a long time as a way of pulling back the curtain and seeing the machinery of the world at work, a process that can help a witch to plan for the future. Casting a set of shells onto a cloth or rolling a set of dice to determine an outcome is not the same as predicting an iron-clad, unchangeable future. Even in the most concrete of divinatory systems, a person might see a potential event coming and make accommodations that eventually prevent or augment that event.

Since the practice of divination involves speaking with complex and limited beings like ancestors or the inner self, the information provided should not ever be taken as absolute fact. Our lives are complicated and messy, new information and experiences are constantly shaping us, and each witch has the ability to change that game at multiple points along the way. *It is one of the tools that we have at our disposal to help us embrace our power to create change.* It is not, and should not be, used to create a sense of helpless fatalism about the future.

The word *game* here is important. If you think about a number of divination systems, you'll notice that many of them are either derived from or have evolved into games of some kind. Tarot has its roots in a game and some obvious connections to playing cards, which are also used for divination. Using coins or dice to cast lots is both a game and a divination tool. The Ouija board, which uses a type of divination involving direct spirit contact, can be purchased in the game aisle of many stores. Even watching for omens is not all that different than road trip games like spotting cars of a specific color or looking for out-of-state license plates.

The link between games and divination is deeply rooted and important. Approaching divination (and all magic) with a sense of play, and willingness to remain authentic and flexible while engaging spontaneously with your imagination, is one of the keys to success. Asking "what if" is at the heart of divination, and at the heart of imaginative play. Play is a liminal space that allows the mind to be creative and powerful. Divination, even when deadly serious, retains a sense of that playfulness that allows us to see magic everywhere.

Systems of Divination

If you are either selecting your first divination system or are curious about trying something new, keep in mind two of the ideas mentioned above: each system has a spirit and ancestry of its own and play is part of divination. An intuitive pull toward a certain system is a great starting place, because you are likely picking up on some of the spirit of that system and sensing your connection. Even if it isn't what you expected, you will likely be rewarded with transformative experience for listening to that call. Each witch will choose differently and that diversity is to be embraced. Divinatory systems are enormously varied with different systems arising from cultures and magical currents the world over.

To work with a method of divination is often to establish a connection with a specific spirit of that tool and always with a line of spiritual ancestry. A palm reader may not be using a specific divinatory tool and a tea leaf reader might use any available tea, saucer, and cup, but all diviners are connecting themselves to the history and cultural context of the method. This is a profound realization if you are a contemporary tea leaf reader, as past readers become connected to you, and their knowledge can be encouraged to flow through your own readings. Magical ancestors through a shared divinatory practice can become a source of power and depth in your practice and research.

The spiritual ancestry of divination is also something to be careful about with regard to culturally appropriative types of divination. Keep in mind that some forms of divination are tied to very deep, often difficult, and tumultuous histories rife with unequal shares of power. Some are considered sacred, closed to outsiders, and intended only for those from within a given culture. I would not discourage you from learning about any open systems when possible, but a real relationship with culturally specific systems outside your own background comes from a rich understanding of the of the system's origin and from respectful engagement with carriers of that culture on their terms. Divination involves play, but it must be matched with empathy, awareness, and respect.

Many witches of the Forest's Edge also choose to work with unique and idiosyncratic systems, such as individual collections of bones and other found objects, allowing for intimate connection with local land spirits. I work with just such a bundle of found objects, including bones, teeth, stones, nuts, seeds, a dried tongue, and even a small wing. I also work with a variation on the Rider-Waite-Smith tarot, and when I read for others, tarot is my tool of choice. But my first divination method, and in fact my entry into magical practice, were the Elder Futhark runes. My personal ramble through divination, gathering methods, is nothing unusual. It is not at all uncommon to work with more than one method or collect several on your journey. Among the hundreds of options, none are better or worse. Play and experiment, but also be ready to dig deep when a system just clicks.

Individual divination methods are abundant, but in general most of the divination we do can be categorized within two types. These broad categories are not at all set in stone, but are more of an illustrative shorthand for making sense of the huge variety of systems. At some level, all divination has an intuitive element. Some systems allow for sweeping flexibility, while others have less wiggle room for individual intuitions. Most witches use some combination of both types.

Observation and Interpretation

Sometimes called *omens and signs*, this type of divination involves the mindful observation of sequences of events that are considered meaningful. Examples include strange births, the activities of animals, shapes found in natural objects, a dream of a certain thing, and weather patterns. The role of the diviner is to *observe* and *interpret* to answer the question. Signs and omens are observed phenomena that are interpreted based on previous experiences, intuition, folklore, and culturally specific meanings. Scrying can be considered part of this category, but instead of externally observable signs, the witch is observing with their inner sight. Witches and other seers are often highly attuned to noticing such things; however, omens can also be broadly observable in a way that allows many people to take notice of them. Many people play divination games in which the shape of an apple peel, the number of petals on a flower, or the next song on the radio is interpreted as an answer to a question.

Casting Lots and Interpretation

Also called *sortilege*, this type requires a physical manipulation of divinatory objects. Sortilege methods are the most common among modern witches and they assign meaning and order to a nearly random outcome through the use of a tool. Cards are pulled from a shuffled tarot pack, leaves stick to a tea cup, and bones or runes are spilled from a container. The way they fall or which cards appear could be described as random, just a lottery, but to the diviner the patterns formed are pregnant with meaning. The role of the diviner is to actively, physically *cast lots* and then to *interpret*. When a witch engages in sortilege, they are acting as not only an observer and interpreter—as in omen reading—but also as a hands-on agent of whatever guiding spirits are the source of the divinatory information. The witch selects the tool, lays out the cloth, draws the circle on the ground, shakes the dice, or suspends the pendulum. In some cases, your choices will be limited, as in systems with "yes" or "no" responses, while other systems allow for detailed, complex responses.

Uses of Divination

Traditional witches use divination in a variety of ways and interpret their tools just as diversely. The use of a divination method of some kind is essential to witchery, but as long as you develop your relationship with the tools and have an ability to use those tools effectively *for you* that's really the goal.

Here are a few different applications for divinatory practices:

1. **Personal Growth:** Many approach divination as a tool for insight into the self. Parts of the self that may need development, acknowledgement, or healing can make themselves visible through divination. We are often half-blind to our own truths, and seeing ourselves and our circumstances clearly can unleash new power. Just because this is about self-knowledge, it doesn't mean that you can't use divination this way for someone else. Much of the professional tarot reading I do for others is of this variety, and friends often ask each other for this kind of reading to get an outside perspective.

2. **Ritual and Priestcraft:** As a way to commune with the gods and sundry other spirits, divination can be a wonderful way of getting a sense of whether a deity or spirit is present, participating, and content. I frequently use divination to find out whether or not a particular offering was accepted by a spirit or deity. In some cases, the use of divination can be its own kind of offering, especially in situations where a spirit has the desire to communicate and the witch provides a voice through the divination tool. Divination tools can also be used to communicate in the other direction—from the witch to the spirits about the witch's intent for a ritual. They can also be used to establish ritual space (as in laying out cards to form a circle around an altar). Using divination in these ways is part of our *priestcraft*, the training by and service to our closest spiritual aids and deities.

3. **Fortune Telling:** As mentioned above, sometimes divination really is about trying to read the future, although just what that means to a particular witch will vary. Some witches may decide that seeing the future is not for them at times, but that is a personal choice.

4. **Spellcasting:** One way of using divination tools, that is absolutely one of my favorites, is as the means of spellwork. Just as you can establish a ritual space by laying out a divinatory tool in a circle in a specific way, you can also select cards, runes, or other divinatory objects that have significant meanings to you and set them up around a burning candle or in a box with a doll or poppet to cause a particular effect. There are frequently tarot cards, runes, or other divinatory objects on my altar to reinforce a spell

    The options for incorporating divination into your spellwork don't have to be solely about the tools themselves but can also help decide whether you should even cast a spell to begin with. If you're already on the fence about casting a spell (especially one that might have unpleasant consequences or outcomes), doing a bit of divination might help you to see the spell a different way.

The magic of divination isn't an isolated part of your practice but part of the woven fabric of your whole practice. Your spellcraft may change or develop as a product of your deepening relationship with divination, or you may find yourself developing specific rituals focused on a particular layout or reading. The roots you put down in each aspect of your practice eventually become the interdependent forest that surrounds you, and those roots intertwine and share with one another, helping to make the whole forest—and the witch—stronger.

Three Tricks to Making Divination Work

There are three tricks for making divination work: learning the language of interpretation, connecting with the tool and its source of knowledge, and inducing a slightly altered state of consciousness.

1. To make any divination system work, you must understand that you are learning a new language. Each and every divination system involves careful, close study of symbols and meanings that you can use to guide your interactions with the spirits, including yourself. And just like learning a new language, divination cannot be learned overnight, and even someone very experienced with tarot may have trouble picking up the I Ching or augury when they first begin. The learning process can be difficult, but the effort lays a solid foundation.

2. In addition to the natural complications of language learning, when you learn to use a divinatory technique you are also building a relationship with the entities or beings on the other end of the pendulum, scrying stone, or crystal ball. So the respectful cultivation of relationship with the tool or technique itself and with the source you're addressing is something successful diviners work at over time.

3. Like all magic, this magic requires a shift in consciousness. To be fair, this is not the radical alteration of hedgeriding or ritual possession but is more akin to the (sometimes) subtler shift of spellcraft. If you've ever tried to piece together a meaningful

tarot card reading by nervously flipping through the little white book that came with the cards, only to find yourself frustrated by a disjointed and uninspiring jumble as your interpretation, then you have felt the experience of reading without the altered state.

The relationship between many divinatory systems and play was mentioned above, and it provides a good entrance into considering the altered state needed here. I would describe it as a looseness, a willingness to let understanding flow so that it can link the pieces together into a meaningful, coherent whole. The notes on inducing altered states in the Creating Ritual and Hedgeriding chapters can apply here. Your way may be different, and you'll know it's a good fit when the interpretations flow and interweave.

Reflections

1. Because divination sometimes seeks to give insight into the future, it begs the question of fate. What does it mean when your divination work suggests a certain outcome in the future? Is it certain? Can you change it?

2. From whom does the insight gained through divination come? What cosmology is *underneath* the divinations you do? Are you aided or helped by any specific entities, or do specific entities respond to you through particular types of divination?

3. What is your history with divination? Is it something you are drawn to? Is it part of your practice already? What methods have you used? How will you use divination going forward?

4. Which kind of divination or divinatory system is most relevant to your sense of spiritual or cultural ancestry? How was it used originally? How is it used now? Do you identify with that divination form, or are there other forms you find more appealing? Why?

5. Is there ever a circumstance in which you would choose not to use divination for ethical reasons? Elaborate, if possible.

6. Under what circumstances are or would you be comfortable doing divination for others? Are there situations in which you would *not* be willing to divine for someone else?

Practice

- Try out forms of divination you haven't before (or don't use very often). This doesn't have to mean embracing other means of divination permanently, but the experimentation can strengthen your understanding of your usual system as well.

- Divine for others, and gather their feedback. Be clear about whether you are telling the future or getting the current lay of the land for the querent (the person asking the question). When you ask for feedback, ask specific questions, like "are there symbols in this system that click with you?" or "what more would you like me to address about your situation in a reading like this?"

- Try using your favorite divination system in a new way. This might mean taking a system you've only ever used to read with and finding practical spellcasting or ritual applications for it.

You might integrate divinatory symbols into other areas of your life—marking runes or ogham staves into food or doing a series of short character sketches based on tarot cards if you're a writer looking for story inspiration.

- Devote yourself to a system. Find a system that really resonates with you and go deep with it. Practice it daily and take notes. Fight with the system and argue back, pointing out where it's not working, and then assessing how you might be able to correct for those sorts of issues. If the system comes from a specific cultural background, do some research and find out more about that culture. Don't just focus on the system, but also learn about the broader history, people, and environment that gave the system its start.

9

THEOLOGY

At the Forest's Edge, we hold no theological dogma, apart from the animism shared by so many. Animism (from Latin *anima*, "breath, spirit, life") in this case just means that everything has a spirit, including plants, mountains, rivers, and animals. The world is alive. Nothing is inanimate and all beings have their own sort of personhood. The human/nature binary is false and creates a painful, disempowering sense of separateness even as it claims to raise us above the rest of nature. We often find ourselves abstracted from our enchanted, lifegiving context, with only a sense of superiority and perhaps duty to keep us warm. Instead, humans are unique and specific, and so is everyone else.

Beyond the affirmation of animism, theologies among witches, and even the members of our tradition are personal and varied. On the subject of the Divine, I encourage each witch to cultivate *a* theology but not *which* theology. It is not required for anyone to believe in either specific polytheistic deities or a universal creator-being to be a witch. Finding where you sit within such a broad range of options is work of course, and it may change over time. But this is another way that traditional witches have both freedom and responsibility. We have the freedom to choose our alliances and allegiances, and to be chosen in return. We have the responsibility to do the work and figure it out, without the comfort of being told how to go about it.

Whichever varieties of deity each witch gravitates toward, if any, we do tend to regard gods as beings that we *work with* rather than as something that dominates or rules over us. As practicing witches, it would make little sense for us to turn over our power and responsibility to a divine being. In this chapter you will find some notes to foster reflection on your own beliefs and those of others. These notes are of course born of my own theological musing and education and should not be held as universal.

On Gods and God

Having wrestled gods and their mysteries for some time now, both academically and personally, I have concluded that the only thing I can say with certainty to define God or gods is that they are or have been worshiped by humans as divine. As soon as I step beyond that definition, I find myself recalling exceptions in this culture or that and things get muddy. Nonetheless, here we go into that muck and mire. When we say deity, god, or goddess, we most commonly mean a supernatural, super-powerful, culturally bound, often-anthropomorphic or partially anthropomorphized figure with a particular domain of powers. When we say the Divine, God, Goddess, or any of a million more poetic appellations, we are shifting our language toward a more amorphous creative force with more universal reach and scope.

There have been times in my life that I have worked more closely with traditional gods than I do now. For many witches, deity work is empowering and the service rendered to a deity flows back toward the witch as gracious blessings. Devotion can have its satisfactions, inwardly and outwardly. That said, I want to own my personal context. I have a terminal graduate degree in Divinity, and I love embracing various roles of spiritual leadership to meet the needs of others. My open-ended view of theology allows for and honors the richness and diversity of theologies I have encountered. However, I don't know if I would say that I work with any gods in solitary practice at the moment. For example, I live in a forest, and it could be said that I work with the god of that very forest. There are similar complexities with figures like Sophia, Mary, and Elen Luyddog, whom I also honor. I see some of my spiritual ancestors in a godlike light at times and see some gods as ancient ancestors. While, as a teacher, I always encourage the development of an individual's ties to deity, my own practice is, well, a bit betwixt and between.

Polytheistic Flavors

Typically, polytheists who worship multiple gods understand those gods to be less than all-powerful, all-seeing, and all-knowing, although sometimes there is also a supreme spirit who exists more removed from humankind. Traditionally each deity is held to be a wholly separate and distinct spiritual being (hard polytheism), although some more mystical or contemporary models hold that each polytheistic deity is an aspect of a single universal creator and sustainer of the universe (soft polytheism). If you identify as a theist of some sort, and many witches do, you may want to affirm or refine your specific beliefs, by asking yourself some of the questions below.

- If your gods are not the creator of everything, then where did they come from? Did they all exist before humans evolved?

- What sustains them? Do they need human belief or offerings? If they don't need them, then why do they want them?

- Did your gods choose you or did you choose them?

- Do you believe in many gods but find yourself called to venerate only one (henotheism)?

- To what degree, if any, do your gods control or influence events on earth? If they do, how do they choose which events to influence?

- What is the relationship amongst gods? What about gods across different cultural pantheons? What about across thematic links (for example, fertility, war, or wisdom)?

- Some of our members identify as panentheists. This means that although they will work with individual deities, they also perceive a universal divine spirit that both suffuses our world and also lies beyond it. How does that notion strike you?

Theological Ancestry and Culture

I poked about at defining deities above because using words is required in a book. However, deities are culturally bound, meaning that not only do specific deities come from within specific cultures—but also, what those cultures mean or meant by the word that we translate as *deity* varies widely. This is to say that if a witch works with a pantheon or individual deities, it is incumbent upon that witch to be respectful and knowledgeable about the broader culture that worships or worshipped those beings. Occasionally this is an easy ask, such as when a witch works with the deities of their own, contemporary broader culture. Often, though, this requires a modern witch to read far beyond the bounds of neopagan texts to understand the cultural and historical matrix surrounding the veneration of their deities. It is well to be mindful of issues of cultural appropriation that may come into play when doing this kind of personal work if the witch is of a dominant culture and is drawn to work with deities of marginalized cultures.

Consider also theological ancestry. Casting back to the Spiritual Ancestry chapter, noting the gods of your forbearers can be a fruitful avenue for your own reflection. That does not mean you have to work with any of their gods, but often it is productive for your ancestor veneration and sense of connectedness through time if you can at least understand your ancestors' gods from their perspectives.

For many modern witches, our recent ancestors followed an Abrahamic religion. However, upon digging and reflecting, you may find that there is more nuance among the past several generations than that. Perhaps there are saints, prominent spiritual leaders, supplemental texts, or angels to which your ancestors were particularly devoted. For example, I connect with my grandmothers and great-greats going way back through their devotion to Mary, the Mother of God, rather than directly through Yahweh (the biblical God). It is frequently the case that even the most ardently Christian (or otherwise monotheistic) ancestors worked with the figures of their faith in a way that would contrast with or even subvert orthodoxy. These peculiar, liminal, theological spaces can be fruitful for witchery. Additionally, reaching back past the spread of Abrahamic faiths, all of our ancestors had different gods, and different gods before that, and so on back to something that likely resembled a primal ancestor veneration and animism. The possibilities for ancestral connection are abundant and multilayered.

Deification and Raising Other Spirits to Godlike Status

A belief held by the early Church Fathers is that of deification, which means for a human to become a god or God as a spiritual goal. Some Christian writers and theological thinkers of various sorts have used this concept somewhat abstractly, while many others have been quite literal. There is a heavier emphasis on this concept in modern Orthodox Christianity than in other branches of Christianity. Humorously, some popular, contemporary Christians criticize "the occult" as being evil specifically due to a doctrine of self-deification seen in some Western occult traditions that have influenced witchcraft, when in fact, deification of humans lies deep within their own Christian tradition as well.

Beyond Christianity, Roman emperors and other leaders could be raised to the level of deification. Those witches with at least a trace of hermeticism in their path will be familiar with deification as a goal in later, Western occult traditions. Contemporary Luciferian and left-hand-path traditions often continue some emphasis on self-deification. Many members of our tradition, and other contemporary traditions of witchcraft, would hold that the gods are ultimately our ancient, powerful ancestors, implying a kind of deification. A New Age belief that has suffused much of the broader culture is that of the Higher Self, an extension of the mundane self that is truer to the fundamentally divine nature of an individual. Mainstream or countercultural, ancient or modern, some idea of deification resounds through many of the streams of narrative, culture, and ethos that likely influence us. As a tradition, we have no universal dogma on the subject, but the notion of deification (for or against) is prevalent enough in world religions and Western occult traditions to be worthy of further consideration.

- What is the relationship between anthropomorphic gods and ancestors?

- Can humans be deified? What does that mean to you?

- How might deification relate to the afterlife?

- Can gods be created?

- Can you temporarily tap into a deified or Higher Self?

Variety and Growth

Within your local witchy community and the modern Pagan community broadly, the questions in this chapter could be answered in ways that reflect impressive diversity. The Divine, broadly speaking, must have relationships with people that differ so vastly that they can seem unrelated or contradictory. Perhaps it is an instance of one deity relating very differently to very different people, or perhaps of more than one distinct deity relating to different people. What is usually necessary—for the sake of community and productivity, is finding a way to be at peace with theological variety.

An excellent starting place for this is to attend to your own spiritual practice and your own relationship with the Divine, however you define it (if you define it). And an excellent next step is to broaden your spectrum of study. Furthering your study will serve the dual purpose of expanding your understanding and perhaps of further inspiring your own practice. I embrace a model of organic growth and change in all things, reflecting the growing, changing world around us, steeped in the enchanting sacred. So allowing your beliefs about a relationship with the Divine to be organic, fluid, and changing reflects that model. We are, after all, at the edge of the forest, where things are not shaded out by heavy canopy cover, nor clear cut and replanted in accord with human logic. Here things develop according to their nature, and the nature of their circumstances, becoming brambles, hedges, and trees in their own right, each in its own way.

Theodicy

The central question of theodicy is how can we reconcile the idea of gods with the existence of enormous pain and suffering? There are many possible approaches to theodicy, but they all begin with our heartfelt questions. For those who maintain any belief in deities, sooner or later we all wonder, why would a super-powerful being *not* stop atrocities? Not all atrocities even, but if there are lots of gods then maybe they could do something about the worst horrors that pertain to their favored people at least. Even if your gods are not all-knowing and all-powerful, why would they not make some effort against child trafficking, genocide, or any number of other blood curdling horrors that plague human and non-human alike. And from a polytheistic perspective—at least stop it when it occurs within their geography, or among their descendants, or the category of human or non-human people they favor. No? Why not? Indifference and individual whims? Powerlessness? If they intervene in our affairs sometimes, but not other times, then what makes the difference? Is it a test? Is it prayer and supplication? Adherence to cultural rules? The benefits or costs to the deity themselves?

This can be tough to consider deeply because we usually want to jump to the defense of our gods and look away from the worst of the worst. There *are* possible answers and those of us who maintain a veneration of deities are absolutely capable of finding those explanations, but to walk a deeper path of witchery includes asking these very dark questions.

Ritual Possession—A Key Skill

In the Forest's Edge way of witchery, ritual possession is an essential skill. This means that the witch allows a spirit being into their body and mind for some purpose. Not all witches start out with this skill. Some find it challenging while others find it slips on readily like worn-in shoes. Not all witches embrace this practice, but we do. If you are coming from an Eclectic Wicca-influenced background then you have heard of *drawing down,* or *drawing down the moon,* in which a high priestess may call her goddess into her body and then speak traditional words as that goddess. Many cultural traditions worldwide have their own specific practices around temporarily hosting spiritual beings within their human selves. As always, your specific sense of spiritual ancestry and cultural ties will inform the tools, language, ritual, spirit beings involved in this process. In truth, to outsiders, this may be one of the strangest things we do. It is peculiar to enact, peculiar to witness, and odd to explain. It is at once a practice of prayerful connection and supplication and simultaneously an assertion of the witch's own inner power and more-than-human nature.

There are a variety of reasons to engage in ritual possession. First and foremost, it allows for a level of connection with a spirit that is not fully available by any other means. It is direct, intimate, and informs not only how you understand the spirit but also how you understand yourself and your relationship to it. Much like with another human, it is one thing to have a conversation but that is not the same as being able to live as that person and see through their eyes. Possession allows the spirit to manifest physically to others witnessing the possession, and, for the witch who is possessed, there is no other way to have such a vivid, visceral, bodily experience coupled with such a wild shift in perspective. Many spirits desire this relationship at least as much as we might. As with all witchery, there are risks to doing deep work, but the rewards of insight, connection, freedom, empowerment, and transformation can be profound.

Possession experiences are most readily thought of as existing within a spectrum. At the fullest, furthest end of the spectrum, the witch's own personality is utterly set aside. If you speak to a witch in this state, you are not speaking to your fellow witch. Often, the witch looks subtly different. Their face looks different because their expressions are uncharacteristic. Their body moves differently. The cadence of their voice is unfamiliar. Their actions may be unpredictable. And then there are the more ineffable changes—they just feel different and you feel different being with them. When a witch in this state speaks, it is not their own thoughts, although their mouth is moving. Often at this level of possession, the witch will have only very vague memories of what is said and done, while other participants in such a ritual can receive messages from the god or other spirit quite directly.

At the lightest or gentlest end of the spectrum would be a sense of being suffused with a spirit, empowered in your work, and perhaps granted some unusual insight, but your own personality is also entirely present. Sometimes it can feel like a mantle settling on your shoulders, a frisson of energy buzzing through your body, or the weight of a headdress on your head, depending on the spirit you're working with. If you speak in this state it is you, with a little something extra. This state is usually easier to slip into for the purposes of spellcraft, because you can continue to follow through with your own plans. It is also readily and safely achieved in solitude. You will be able to remember what you have done and said. There is no major risk, only a little giving up of control.

In between these states are an endless variety of shades of grey. None of it is better or worse, it's more about what you are comfortable with and hope to achieve. It is also entirely normal to move along the spectrum during the course of a ritual possession experience. For example, in a possession experience with a group, the one possessed might later describe that there were times when they were gone or when they absolutely *were* the spirit and other times when it felt more like having a very close connection to the spirit and relaying what they would like to say. To slip in and out of these states is normal. To mostly maintain one state is also normal. It all counts.

This is rarely an issue for a practiced witch, but it is worth a mention that beings who might partner with us in ritual possession run the gamut of temperament, as do all beings. Not all deities, ancestors, fae, sundry spirits share your living-human sense of ethics. Not all share your goals. It is well to remember that a witch is not a helpless slave to a god or to any being. We are powerful and in case a god forgets the human notion of consent, we ourselves can remember. In any ordinary healthy relationship you have boundaries regarding how you are willing to be treated and how you choose to engage. The same should go for a spiritual relationship involving ritual possession. There is an element of release and letting go in possession, but that experience stands on a firm foundation of a bounded relationship and a pragmatic understanding of the spirit in question.

At a practical level, you already have the skills you need to induce ritual possession. It requires the induction of an altered state of consciousness and intention-driven, purposeful letting go, just as hedgeriding does. It requires building a strong and mutual relationship with a spirit being, just as we animist witches do when communing with spirits. To do it intentionally requires a focus and firmness of purpose, just as spellcasting does. Optionally, it can be fostered through well constructed ritual, just as other witchy experiences often are. At its conclusion, the witch must ground themselves in this reality and recenter their own spirit.

To outline the general flow of the process when done intentionally:

1. First, build a strong relationship with a spirit, communing with them through whatever means you choose. Typically, they will indeed want to engage in a ritual possession with you and it is through your relationship with them that the purpose of possession will emerge.

2. Prepare in practical terms for your experience—with ritual attire, tools, instruments, written words, and the like.

3. Begin a ritual for possession with your usual ritual opening, followed by honoring and making offerings to the spirit.

4. Next, honor yourself in some way that builds connection with this specific spirit. Popular options include anointing with oils or infusions; donning a mask, headdress, veil, or something similar. There may also be blessings laid on the witch by other participants, if any. This step and the previous step may involve considerable ritual theatre, or very little.

5. Next, explicitly invite the spirit into yourself and clarify your intent for the experience. You are the host offering hospitality.

The Witch at the Forest's Edge

6. Then, induce an altered state of consciousness through whatever means are relevant and effective. Let go and run with it. It will end in its own time.

7. Afterwards, give thanks, ground yourself, and replenish your body, as usual.

Above I have outlined a highly ritualized version of this practice. Often for those who are newer to the practice that is the most effective way to try it. With that said, especially for the lighter end of the spectrum with a very familiar spirit, there is often little outward ritual. It is just an inward shift. It is also sometimes possible or preferable to try possession while hedgeriding. In other words, it may be useful to practice possession *there* rather than *here*. There are a couple reasons why—perhaps because the work you are doing while possessed must be done in the Otherworld or because for some witches who hedgecross easily, it may be easier or more comfortable to have already flown from the physical body. However, limiting possession *only* to a hedgecrossed state misses part of the wonder and power of the visceral, embodied element.

Reflection

1. Do you believe in or work with any gods? How has this changed over time, if it has?

2. Does the Divine, as you experience it, change as the world changes, or does it remain static through time?

3. Is the Divine omniscient, omnipotent, omnipresent? If not, how much agency does the Divine as you experience it possess?

4. What role, if any, does the Divine have in ongoing creation and in original creation?

5. Is the Divine's relationship with humankind different from the Divine's relationship with the rest of the world and other living things? If so, how?

6. When truly terrible, unjust things happen either at a personal or societal level, is the Divine in that?

10

A GREEN AND
LOCAL CRAFT

As I write in the attic of my forest cottage, snapping turtles slide through dark mud, and matted spots of fern and forb show where deer have bedded down. Limestone looks down from its steep outcroppings, releasing a trickle of spring water that has enjoyed the hospitality of stone on its endless journey. I am part of this community. My home here in the forest is one home among many. I dwell not on a lonely pedestal of culture above and against my other-than-human neighbors, but as one integral part of the neighborhood. To know my neighborhood, or my bioregion, is to gradually develop relationships that reflect the ecological reality, enrich the ecological systems, and empower my magic.

Here, at the Forest's Edge, our witchcraft is a green witchcraft. Being green goes ever so far beyond liking nature, studying herbalism, or composting, although all are worthy and green pursuits. Green witchcraft is about relationship, integrity, and interconnectedness. Our view of the world as richly alive and spirit-filled can be described as a kind of personalism, which means that the world is full of persons, only some of whom are human. Just like human persons, everyone else is both a distinct individual and related to others. Some spirits are injured and angry, some are disinterested, and some are open and curious.

While the theological proposition of animism is discussed in more length in the Theology chapter, here we simply call our hearts to beat with the seasons. We work our magic deeply entwined with the enspirited world enfolding us. We strive to keep a dynamic balance of give and take, for all of nature can be both glorious and terrible. We emphasize integrity among the various aspects of our lives and avoid creating false dichotomies between material and spiritual or human and natural. We know we are part of the rhythms and cycles of nature, so we mark them with celebrations. We are both ferociously wild and graciously domestic in our greenness. Indeed, all we do arises from a green perspective. This chapter is presented as an additional gateway into reflecting very intentionally on the green, localized nature of your own craft.

A Deeper Shade of Green

A green and local craft does not belong only to witches who live in rural areas or who count their property in acres. It does not belong only to those who take extended backwoods journeys or who cultivate enormous gardens. I may currently be the archetypal witch in the woods, but I haven't always been. Most of my life has been spent elsewhere, and I created and completed my first bioregional worksheet for teaching witchcraft when I lived in an apartment building with a view of more apartment buildings. Your circumstances do not separate you from the spirits of the land, because simply by existing you are part of nature. The choice to practice as a green and local witch is available to everyone.

Sometimes, green witchcraft is simply equated with a knowledge of magical herbalism. The *green* in our green witchery does not just refer to plants but to all of nature. Sometimes, practices (like herbalism) are a major outgrowth of that connection, and sometimes not. Herbalism (whether for spellcraft, healing, or trance induction) can be a very valuable part of that practice, but a green witch interested in herbalism would endeavor to know and work collaboratively with the persons or spirits of their herbs. Herbalism is just one example here, but the principles of respect, communication, and reciprocity hold true when working with animals, minerals, weather, and *genus loci.*

A green witch connects to the world directly, not just symbolically, beginning where the witch lives. It is a fine thing to memorize the symbolic significance for oak wood, but it is another thing to get to know the oak tree in your backyard, or the oak-hickory forest ecosystem that dominates your region. This intimate knowledge tends to ensure that we do not develop an abstract or idealized view of nature as something pristine and apart from ourselves that can get in the way of real relationships. Similarly, it is good to love humankind as an ethical stance, but it is another thing to love your friend, spouse, child, or neighbor in such a way that you know and honor that person's peculiarities, strengths, and histories. Getting local and specific will inevitably shape your craft. For example, if you spend time studying the plants in your location, you may find that most commonly mentioned herbs in the perennially popular witchy books do not naturally grow in your region and some may be invasive or hard to cultivate. So connecting to the wild, native, and readily cultivated plants in your area can be a fiercely different experience from basing your practice on studying a popular book.

Although the spirits of nature are literally everywhere, many have long been silent, or have been so horribly abused that they retreat or grow hostile. Also, like a human being, no individual place or other-than-human-being is an island. Each being is relational or ecologically entwined with others at its core. This is to say that if you accept the real individuality of those who are not human, your efforts to know them cannot be mere formalities or one-sided performances. To work with an enspirited world is to be a good listener as well. If a particular boulder is silent despite your overtures, it doesn't lack a spirit; it lacks an interest in you. If you sense hostility or trickiness, believe your senses and the spirits. You may try to work through the issue, or you might turn elsewhere. The world is enchanted and full of wonder, but that does not mean that all weather is mild sunshine or that everyone is suitable to be your friend.

Once a green witch has made the effort to get to know the beings in their home and neighborhood and has developed a talent for seeing and listening beyond the physical, they may be sought out by nature spirits in a variety of places. It then becomes a matter of discerning which are helpful, which need help, and which just want to be recognized.

Many Voices

Every potted plant, tiny backyard, and tree on the corner has its own spirit and also likely holds a bit of the essence of the category to which it belongs. Or, to put it differently, we are not the only ones with spiritual ancestry. All willows of a particular species, for example, have evolved similar biological and ecological properties through their ancestral lineage, as well as having a set of folkloric, magical, and medicinal properties in their species' ancestral relationship with humans and other animals. They also have a familial relationship with other species of willows that have some related and some distinct characteristics. Yet each willow will also have a unique personality. Learning about one is often the best gateway into the other.

Some green witches prefer to learn about the biological, ecological, folkloric, medicinal, and magical properties of a type of plant (or animal or mineral . . .), and then seek an introduction to a particular individual of that plant, while some start by getting to know the specific plant and later expand their knowledge of the type of plant. Both are valid ways of connecting with natural spirits of all kingdoms.

Although categorizing spirits whom we barely understand is a hazardous undertaking, it can be helpful to draw a few gentle distinctions. Using my forest as an example, I see each fern, paw-paw, and millipede as having a spirit. As mentioned above, each also has a connection, similar to spiritual ancestry, to its forebearers, and overarching category. Beyond this though, I relate to the forest as a whole. This grander sort of spirit that encompasses many individual spirits is sometimes called a *genus loci*, or a spirit of a place that is greater than the sum of its parts. Sometimes these spirits of place are seen to have a particular form to our perception (a troll-like being, an especially sentient tree, an antlered humanoid, or other form) and sometimes they do not take a form of their own. The spirit of a place is a unique being unto itself, with a personality that builds and changes over time, shaped by its experiences.

So, this gives us individual spirit beings and collective spirits of place, but categories also become more complex when the lore of particular cultures or places is introduced. Maybe you live near a river where someone drowned and their spirit has become something like a human-flavored genus loci. Maybe there's a forest whose spirits were historically described as elf-like beings. Are those beings fairies? Genus loci? Probably both to some extent, but you see the way complexities can grow. It's part of the liminal charm of dealing with those who keep to the shadows and evade the notice of many.

Going Local

To gain a rooted sense of place, we observe, study, and forge a working relationship with the locally specific water cycle, tides, plants and animals (native and introduced), fungi, geology, seasons, weather patterns, and human history. In this way, the green witch's practice becomes an expression of the land under our feet, the sky above our heads, and the water surrounding and infusing us. Like all people do, your local land changes with time, and so will your relationship change and evolve.

The place that you relate with most intimately need not literally be your own street, backyard, or garden, although that is a good starting place for connecting with your ecoregion. It could also begin with a nearby woodland, sea cliff, creek, or urban park. Everywhere has a spirit of place and it is our work to connect with that spirit collectively and those spirits individually through both knowledge and practice.

Your Spirit Senses and Intuition

Being a green witch, like being any kind of magical practitioner, takes work, and one of the most difficult things about this particular type of craft is that it requires the practitioner to be very attentive to their intuition and spirit senses. It can be hard to listen to your gut instincts even just in day-to-day matters, but when it comes to the Craft, many people feel doubly uncertain. Green witchcraft isn't about bucking all of the wisdom and traditions of formal magical paths, but it also isn't about tidy, memorizable rules about the right and wrong way to do things. The practice of every green witch is highly personalized because we learn and practice in part by trial and error and by listening to the very specific voices of *local* nature and the voice within.

It's not that a green witch just makes things up wily-nily. We learn these things through direct experience and study. A green witch spends time just sitting with a plant, for instance, and touching, tasting, and smelling it. They ask the spirit of the plant to grant knowledge about its properties. This knowledge absolutely should be considered in conversation with the wisdom of science, folklore, and the like, but especially when it comes to magic; the green witch's guidance from specific nature spirits—which often communicate through the spirit senses and intuition—are central, experiential sources.

The Street Where You Live

The best way to get started on the path of the green witch is to get outside in your own yard and neighborhood. Familiarizing yourself with the plants, minerals, and wildlife, while paying attention to the changes in the weather and the local seasons, grounds you in your specific locality and enables you to start learning about and tapping into the spirit of the land you live on. Even if you live in a densely human-populated city, you are still living on the earth and within a natural web, and you can have a relationship with the spirits who surround your home. It's easy to lose sight of the wonder and magic around us all the time, but it's important to remember that every place on earth is special, powerful, and sacred.

Begin by noticing things that may have gone unmarked before. When it rains, where does the water run? Does a species of mushroom keep popping up under the shrub in front of your apartment building? Which way do clouds and weather usually move? Have you kept a list of the birds you see around your home? (It's probably not just pigeons, although they are worthy of appreciation, too.) Even if not so much as a blade of grass is visible, the foundation of your home is rooted in the underlying soil and geology and, by extension, so are you. You've probably already noticed some of these things, so give yourself credit. Most likely you already know where the sun rises and sets and how your home is oriented to the directions.

Your Home, Itself

In addition to the external aspects of your dwelling place, your home may have an indwelling spirit or spirits of its own. These house spirits may or may not be directly linked to the surrounding and underlying land, but, in my experience, they are, at least in part. They have also been shaped by previous dwellers and sometimes were brought from a different homeland by immigrating families. And of course nothing could be more local. The notion of house spirits pervades various cultures, with different names and characteristics, and you may want to explore the house spirit lore connected to your sense of spiritual ancestry. You may also find that you can call the building itself to wake from its slumber and become an active ally. After all, lumber was once great trees, metal and brick were once of the soil, and your home can remember where it comes from and what it has seen—once it has a witch who will listen and engage.

The Wild Green Yonder

Of course, to fully appreciate all of the aspects of the earth and to practice working with a wide variety of energies and spirits, it can help to get out and see the wider world, too. Trips to the local park, nearby bodies of water, and national forests help further the green witch's education and experience, and deepen an appreciation for the natural web of life. In particular, if your home is in a watershed for a body of water, getting to know that body of water is not a long trip, but it can be very significant. And trips to places of great power, where many have worshiped or natural phenomena intensify the earth's power, are also wonderful experiences. At the very least, retreating to more secluded natural environments may eliminate some of the distractions brought about by the people with whom we share our living spaces. However, at the end of the day, it is important to realize that everything that can be known and achieved at Stonehenge or Yellowstone can in some way be learned and practiced in your own backyard. See the world, but start at home.

Taking the First Steps

The first steps toward a deeper shade of green lie in acknowledging your desire to know the spirits and gain intimacy. It is all about starting small and sticking with it. Begin opening yourself up to the messages and lessons of the natural world, and let it be known to the spirits around you that you wish to build a relationship with them. Our path is one of experiential learning, and you will find that the more you immerse yourself in working with the spirits of the earth, the more momentum you will build. Apprentice yourself to your place. The Craft you construct may not look exactly like anyone else's, and that's okay—honor the information that you gather through your own connections with the world. The most important thing to remember is that the power of the green witch lies in the relationship with all that is sacred, grand, and humble.

A Witch's Cycles and Holidays

If you're at all familiar with the eight seasonal sabbats celebrated by most contemporary Pagans, you might be surprised that for all my emphasis on local specificity, we celebrate these holidays at the Forest's Edge as well. Less surprising, is the emphasis on reinterpreting these holidays in light of your local seasons. We also observe both dark (new) and full moons. These points are ways to connect regularly with the rhythms of the solar seasons and the lunar cycles while also remaining connected with the broader communities of Paganism and witchcraft. Humans crave a connection to rhythm and we just love to mark time with holidays, and that becomes most meaningful when it has a connection to communal traditions as well.

A holiday, whether a full moon or the autumnal equinox, is a single point marked out in an ongoing cycle. Moon phases and seasons are ever changing, and by creating holidays, we create thresholds, liminal spaces between one part of the cycle and the next. A holiday is a crossroads, suspended between the paths leading up to it and the paths leading away. This is a tremendously powerful place to stand as witch and can be worked with to great effect. However, rote celebration of seemingly irrelevant holidays can become more hollow than holy. Each witch or group has the most to gain by celebrating holy days that are culturally or locally specific and by celebrating the eight sabbats and the moons in a way that fits with lifestyle, local seasons, and cultural practices. It is more important to honor the cycles of nature in a way that is authentic to your location and sense of spiritual ancestry than to do what is done by others.

Eight Sabbats and Seasonal Holidays

It's true that acknowledging time and nature via the calendar marked by others before us has the additional power of connecting us to the spiritual ancestors and so can result in more levels of meaning and an even deeper sense of connection. It may also be the case that if you live in a place without four seasons, adapting the holidays to your bioregion and lifestyle could prove infeasible. Prioritizing local witchery is absolutely valid, and you can let go of the eight holidays. It's also possible that you are deeply immersed in a culture very much apart from these holidays and that's also good. Because we are inherently part of nature, I do think that having a regular cycle of holidays is a good way to live with the rhythm of the seasons, so that may involve some delicious opportunities for creativity on your part.

A quick Internet search can provide a starting point for those who are unfamiliar with the observance of the eight sabbats. For those who wish to reshape these sabbats to better reflect local seasons, one way to do so begins by looking carefully at conventional descriptions. Take any sabbat and see what seasonal or agricultural markers are mentioned. Then, take careful note of what is happening at that time of year in your area and experiment with integrating different symbolism. For example, Imbolc or Candlemas is often linked to the pregnancy and lactation of ewes (from the meaning of the word Imbolc), however if you live in an area where there are no sheep, or in a warmer or colder climate than the rather mild Irish climate, the lactation of ewes may not be a meaningful symbol for you. So, look both to the conventional lore for the holiday and what is happening in your region, your garden, and your home and begin to fine-tune a meaning that resonates for you.

Around here, at that time of year daffodil stalks are emerging, there may be a couple of the tiniest spring wildflowers in a sheltered part of the forest, and the hawks are pairing up loudly. It's very cold, usually cloudy, and we often harvest young roosters around this time, leaving this grey holiday spattered in vivid red. Nothing to do with sheep here, although the blessing of candles in the cold grey feels very salient. It is both a dark and difficult time as the novel charm of winter is waning, and a time for candles and the blooming of one brave little flower sure to be killed by frost.

You may find that as you link sabbats more closely with your experience of the living world around you, you will be more enthusiastic about celebrating them because they feel more relevant to your experience. This is why I suggest that if you don't like a particular sabbat, before you drop it entirely, examine the ways its typical celebration may be a dreadful misfit for the rhythms of your life. If it isn't an equinox or solstice, moving the holiday slightly to better match your region can help. Otherwise, reshaping what exactly that holiday marks and means can be a solution to keep the community connection and make it meaningful.

Lunar Cycles

While the sabbats are arrayed across the annual cycle of seasons created by our planet's relationship to the sun, we witches are ever entwined with the moon. At the Forest's Edge, we track the cycles of the moon as do most witches, with the full moon being a time for fulfillment, creation, and outward focus, and the dark or new moon being a time for ancestors, inner work, and release. The waning moon aligns with decrease, banishing, and release, while the waxing moon is a time of increase, growth, and building. Wherever you are, the moon is there, and finding your way of relating to lunar cycles can be a very important part of your path.

Witches' Rest

In addition to sabbats and moons, we honor the concept of the Witches' Rest. Some consider the Rest period to be from Samhain to winter solstice, ending when the sun begins it gradual ascent. This model prioritizes solar cycles and symbolism. Meanwhile, others may focus on the period from midwinter to Candlemas/Imbolc as Rest because that tends to be the coldest time of year with the least evident life outdoors and the fewest gardening or agricultural tasks in many temperate climates. It is also after the rush of the holiday season. This latter timing works best with my life and local seasons.

In the southern hemisphere or two-season climates, when exactly is the quietest, most inward time will vary as well. Either way, finding your Rest offers a dark, quiet, reflective time, a time of the void and the underworld. Rest is a time to sink in and recharge. We see this practice as a reflection of and a way of syncing with the world around and inside us. Each individual witch can find a personal way to Rest that fits authentically with their own life. The concept of Witches' Rest aligns with the seasons or solar cycle in a similar way as the dark moon aligns with the lunar cycle. Both Rest and the dark moon carry similar symbolism and both can be appropriate for similar kinds of work.

The Greening and Other Annual Habits

In addition to regular holidays and as-needed workings, we at the Forest's Edge find a way to reach out at least once per year to other local nature spirits with a very intentional goal of healing and giving back. Of course, these are ongoing relationships not remotely limited to once a year; however, it can help to have at least one planned time that is unrelated to asking for help or achieving a human goal— one that is entirely focused on giving to and healing our other-than-human neighbors. This is called the Greening. This could take a practical form (a beach clean-up or planting a meadow of bee-friendly flowers, for example) or could be more magical in nature (like a healing for an ignored and wounded spirit in an urban neighborhood). I also encourage all who are able, to engage in a practice of ritual possession at least once per year. It may well be that either or both of these types of practice feature in your work far more often than once a year. But I have found that scheduling these two activities helps keep them in the busy witch's repertoire leading to more frequent organic workings of this sort as well. It's a bit like establishing a good habit.

Sense of Place and Ancestry

When your spiritual ancestry is rooted in a land other than your current ecoregion, a creative tension can develop. Questions can come up around celebrating holidays in accordance with local seasons or in accordance with ancestral traditions from a different climate. Other areas where ancestral and local ecoregions may offer differences can lie in folklore, lifestyles, native plants, animals, and geology. Neither impulse is wrong and both are traditional—to want to connect to the lands and practices of ancestors and to want to reflect a deeply local rootedness.

These places of tension can also be places for creativity and communication to blossom. Each witch must encounter and work through these places in a meaningful way by speaking and working directly with the ancestors and other-than-human-persons within their web. As green witches, we honor our other-than-human kinship ties. This can be envisioned as a horizontal web extending through space. As ancestral witches, we honor human historical and cultural ties of genealogical and spiritual ancestry. This can be envisioned as a vertical web extending through time. However, there are still more layers to these interconnections. For example, our other-than-human kin in our local areas have ancestries that are deeply entwined with human presence. For example, a patch of land in an urban neighborhood may once have been agricultural land worked by indigenous peoples, and before that it may have been a broadleaf forest. Our web of interconnection is incredibly complex, chaotic, and multidirectional—in such a way that in truth the ancestral and green aspects of our craft are one and the same.

For those of us navigating this terrain of competing needs, who are the descendants of settlers on indigenous land, it is important to remember that appropriation of indigenous traditions and sacred spaces is not the answer. Cultivating a path that is an authentic reflection of your web of relationships through time and space is.

Reciprocity and Greening

Mentioned briefly above, green witches in our tradition envision themselves as doing a special kind of work or craft—sometimes called the Greening of the Earth—which is a way of saying that we participate in tending to and healing the natural world. This can be done literally by tending a garden, removing litter from a shoreline, caring for animals, and the like. But the greening of the earth also refers to the green witch's efforts to establish a connection to the spirits of nature that have been forgotten, abused, or ignored by so much of society for so long. Our work involves actively healing the relationship between humans and the other spirits of nature as a community, as well as working to restore the physical state of the planet. So in a way, the Greening of the Earth refers to the healing of the earth on all levels—physical and spiritual—and this is fundamental to the green witch's practice.

As a spiritual practice, the general principles of communing with spirits apply here. The time you spend with other nature spirits is key to developing a relationship. Try to approach by listening, not talking. What is needed here? Is your help acceptable? The sense of connection and puzzle pieces fitting into place may be immediate or a more long-term project. Making simple offerings when passing through an area makes sense, but in your immediate area or where you feel very deeply connected, being regular, spending quiet time there, giving concrete help when possible and spiritual energy otherwise are appropriate. In those places of very deep connection, significant offerings are appropriate to solidify a uniquely deep mutual relationship, not unlike a marriage.

Beyond the magical practice, many witches worry about being eco-friendly enough in their day-to-day lifestyle. The cultivation of personal integrity and the integration of our craft into all aspects of life does imply doing work that reflects our beliefs. It's true, we tend to do things like using organic or permacultural gardening practices, conserving energy, reusing materials, and supporting local agriculture. These actions are ways of walking our talk or cultivating integrity and integration of our craft. This does not in any way mean that any of us are close to perfect in our eco-friendly efforts, nor that we judge ourselves or others harshly. But it does mean that we care and actively work at it as we are able, one step at a time. We strive for what is both helpful and joyful because that is how friendships grow. Local wines are both delicious and the blood of the land. Cleaning up a local creek offers a beautiful creek walk, a reciprocal magical relationship with the creek, and environmental benefits. Integrity will look different for each witch, and the balance between those actions that can be seen (like reusing or repairing materials) and those that likely cannot be seen by others (like listening to the spirits of your land) is ever evolving, particular, and peculiar to each witch.

Reflection

1. How is your practice currently green?

2. How would you like to further green your practice?

3. What is your ecoregion? An ecoregion (similar to a bioregion) is a characteristic pattern of ecosystems in a geographical area. It is a place's signature household of animals, plants, weather, water, and geology. You'll want to get as granular, small-scale, and local as you can with this. For Americans, the EPA, the

National Wildlife Federation, US Forest Service, and USGS web sites can be excellent starting places for locating your ecoregion. See the resources section for URLs.

4. Are there any examples in your life of differences between ancestral and local ecoregions? How have you navigated them so far? What are you still sorting out?

5. Complete the questionnaire that begins on page 147.

6. What are some local sayings, ghost stories, festivals, or legends?

Practice

- **Create a full spirit of place profile:** Select an area that is dear to you, most likely the region or part of the region where you live (for example, the inner Nashville basin or the cedar glade ecosystem) and create a profile of its history and ecosystem. Your answers to the eco-regional quiz (page 147) can form the foundation of the profile. Include sections describing boundaries, geology, water flow and features, flora and fauna, seasonal and weather information, and relevant histories of human settlement and land use.

- **Start a focused observation journal:** Select one specific spot to observe over time. The spot could be a portion of your backyard, a special place in a meadow, or an old tree stump. Keep a written journal of what goes on there and how it changes over time. The smaller the spot, the more detailed you can get. Note all of the details you can find: moisture level, texture, decomposition processes, colors, growth, insect activities, animal droppings, and so on. You will want to maintain this practice through at least one change of seasons. The journal need not be eloquent or lengthy, but should be regular.

- **Bond one-on-one:** Intuitively determine a particular being, found in your local area, to which you are called. This could be a tree, a rock formation, a body of water, or a type of animal. Try building a reciprocal relationship with it. Observe it in person. Read about that type of being in terms of folklore, biology, ecology, magic, and medicine. Practice sensing its energy. Ask for dreams about it. Do divinations. Make offerings to it. Give it space to feel you out. Ask what it wants or if it needs any healing. Once the basis of a relationship has been forged, hedgecrossing to work with its spirit and spellwork with its aid can form deeper working bonds.

- **Connect with commercial materials:** Often in green witchcraft, we work with plant and animal spirits that are either found locally or, particularly in the case of plants, that we have carefully cultivated ourselves. But often enough we also find ourselves drawn to or in need of a plant, stone, or animal that is not found locally. Most commonly, perhaps, we find this when we purchase commercially produced dried herbs, so that will be used as an example here (although the same can be true of wood, bone, feathers, and stones). Because we regard the herb as having a distinct spirit in addition to its symbolic value and because we regard it as part of a larger web, we are obliged to relate to the herb in a lively, spiritual way, not just as a dead ingredient. How each witch does this is not mandated. You must find your own way. Likely the first step is to energetically sense the material—does it feel dead or empty or sleeping to you or can you still sense a connection to living spirit? How strong is that spirit? What does it need? Once you have assessed the situation, you may find that simply working with it as you had intended is enough. Or you may sense a need to call back or awaken the spirit of the being.

- **Ask permission:** Of course as witches, we often choose to do magical and ritual workings out of doors and regard the land we work with as sacred and spirit filled. We also do things like asking a tree for permission before taking a branch. It is a good idea to ask the specific spirits of a ritual location for their permission to use that space for that purpose. This practice tends to be very interesting when done in a wild place that is less accustomed to humans and where you do not commonly practice. If you normally practice in a spot in your yard, you likely have already established a working relationship there. A wilder place is more apt to tell you "No!"—or conversely to be quite curious and engaged in your work. If this practice is new for you, one place to begin is to go to your chosen location and reach out your senses to all the beings within your planned circle—from trees to soil fungi to ants—ask for permission and blessing, and be open to the response. A divination tool can also be used. The Communing with Spirits chapter will also help you develop further relationships.

- **Practice sensing:** In a way, this is a fundamental practice. Center yourself and then reach outward to the natural world in the small area around you, far beyond the things you can physically see. Extend your awareness from the tiniest microorganism to the rabbit in their burrow to the plants of the underbrush to the bees buzzing by to the soil itself and the water it holds.

Take your time, sensing the many, many layers of being around you. Sense how they work together in one enormously complex ecosystem. See if you can go from perceiving each individual being to hearing them as one voice—all the many beings and the land itself as one dynamic, living spirit who is as aware of you as you are of it.

• **Explore your wheel:** Draw three circles on a piece of paper. Around one of the circles, write the names and dates of the sabbats and other holidays you personally recognize or wish to recognize as a witch. Around the second circle, write the phases of the moon. Around the third circle, write the cycle of the day however you identify it. Go back to each circle and try to write at least three associations with each thing you have written down—maybe a seasonal object, maybe a practice, maybe a food, or maybe something that you have observed in your own environment. Perhaps even something as personal as "this is when I have the most energy" or "this is when I feel most witchy." Work with these wheels—how do they overlap? How do they turn in your daily life and practice? How can you live them more intentionally, and personalize them more?

• **Name the moons:** Sometimes the thirteen full moons in a year are given names that reflect seasonal occurrences at that time. This is an ancient practice reflected in names both from European cultures and from a number of Native American nations. For example, depending on where you live, the full moon in June might be called the Strawberry moon because that's about the time that strawberries are ripe there. This creates thirteen mini-seasons following a lunar calendar. Name the moons where you live to create your own lunar calendar.

- **Write a brief, magically ecological description of your home:**
  Attend to the aspects that most directly resonate with you or
  affect your witchcraft. For example a person might note things
  like, "My ranch-style home, built in 1950, is based around
  a large fireplace of bricks likely made in Texas. This hearth is
  often a focal point of my witchery. Grounded in limestone
  bedrock, the soil is loamy and slightly basic. Originally this
  area was oak-hickory forest and a hunting ground for the Creek
  nation. Nestled between the shelter of an eighty-year-old east-
  ern white pine, who is the guardian and keystone spirit of this
  place, and my own gardens. My home is also less than a mile
  from a medium-sized creek that runs fast in the winter, slow in
  the summer. Bounded by mossy banks, the creek has a curious
  and engaging spirit. I plan to work more with this creek when
  I am doing water-related magic. Between its history as a forest
  and present as suburban yard, the spirits of this place were
  often ignored or abused by depleting agricultural practices, and
  I am working magically with the land spirits and practically
  with soil-regenerating gardening practices to foster healing."

A Questionnaire for Cultivating Sense of Place

1. Trace the water that you drink from precipitation to tap.

2. What kind of soil is under your feet here? Is it sandy, clay,
   rocky, silt, something else? What about the underlying rock?

3. Name five native edible plants in your region and the seasons
   they are harvested.

4. How long is the growing season (from frost to frost)?

5. What month or season has the most rainfall in your area? Which is the driest?

6. Name five birds that live in your area. Which are migratory and which are year-around residents?

7. What is the land use by humans during the past two centuries? (The narrower the better: you learn more from the history of a city lot or a single plot of land than from a large area.)

8. Where does your garbage ultimately go?

9. From what direction do winter storms generally come in your region?

10. What geological events and processes shaped the land where you live?

11. If you live near the ocean, when is high tide today? If you live near a lake, pond, river, or creek, how is its water level right now—high, low, or average?

12. When do the deer rut in your region, and when are their young born?

13. What spring wildflower is consistently among the first to bloom where you live?

14. Name four grasses in your area. Are any of them native?

15. What are the major plant associations in your region? (A plant association is a group of plants that normally grow in the same ecological zone, such as the Tallgrass Prairie.)

16. How recently was the moon full?

17. Where does your electric power come from and how is it generated?

18. Where is there wilderness in your bioregion?

19. What are the primary sources of pollution?

20. What are the major natural sounds you are aware of in any particular (name it) month or season?

21. Where is the nearest earthquake fault? When did it last move?

22. How far are you above sea level?

23. What are the seasons where you live and which months do they typically encompass?

11

THE PRACTICAL USE OF
MAGICAL THEORY

We pluck tender leaves with whispered thanks, leaving precious trinkets beneath old trees. Words leap from our mouths, speaking power into the world. Our bodies dance to exhaustion and our voices chant to hoarseness. Our eyes shut and our breath slows as we sink into the earth and our spirits fly. Ink trails across paper. Secrets are tucked into tiny bags, and the white of bone glows in the moonlight as we read for wisdom. Magic!

When you think of magic, do you think first of wands, cauldrons, and charms written on bits of parchment? Most of us do. Many of us were raised on Hollywood magic. In truth, though, magic is much bigger than casting spells. The forest's edge, as a liminal place, is a place suffused with magic. Magic is enchantment made purposeful. The purpose of magic is *change*, external or internal, in this world or others. The word magic encompasses a variety of the practices of witches, including the obvious spellwork. You may not be equally excellent at every kind, and that's just fine.

Whatever your magical niche, it's a peculiar thing being a magic worker in a culture that considers real magic evil at worst and a fantasy at best. But then, it has long been a peculiar thing. Since the time of Ancient Greece, magic was often the suspect, illicit work of outsiders. By and large since then in Western culture, the dominant religions are the only legitimate sources of magic-like practices. Anyone working at the edges of those boundaries, beyond the control of the hierarchy, is considered a magic worker and therefore highly suspect. Sometimes, the language of magic has been used with approval but more often with disapproval—not because it doesn't work but because it does. Since the enlightenment, magic workers are more often regarded as primitive, inferior, irrational, foreign, and exotic in comparison to the superior, contemporary Western religions. Now there is more of an understanding that this way of thinking is ethnocentric and built on false categories and assumptions, but it hasn't changed society at large. In the language of the '90s movie, *The Craft*, "We are the weirdos, mister."

What does it mean that magic workers are outsiders? It positions us nicely in the liminal space between the nucleus of mass culture and the realms beyond. We've always straddled this line between being admired and needed and feared and disowned. The language of *witch* places our magic even more firmly at the margins—even among magic workers that term stands out. With that word, we reclaim the power of doing magical work that is not socially sanctioned by dominant powers. As witches and magic workers, we do well to embrace this aspect of our identity and remember that we are aligned with other marginalized groups.

When we do these peculiar things we call magic, what exactly are we *doing*? Is it real? Where does magic come from and how do you work with it most effectively? Whether or not you presently have a fully fledged theory of magic, is, in the hands-on, practical sense, neither here nor there. You do the work and it works. Or sometimes—for us all—you do the work and it fails.

You and your ancestors may not always have had the luxury of time to ponder *why* when you are driven by *need*. However, there is room for us to take our work a step further. Magic is a mystery appreciated through direct experience. To consider how it works is not like the explanations of science, nor is it meant to reveal the mystery. The theories herein are useful ideas about practice and a transparency about the notions that underlie the work. A close consideration of the implicit hows and whys can light some pathways to continued development and refinement of your skillset. The three categories below are based on a magic practioner's perspective, and are influenced in part by the work of Frater U.D. I prefer these categories to those derived from anthropology and psychology because I believe that these categories are inherently practical for a person who is practicing magic as a modern witch. After all, my goal in this writing is not to theorize about the past or to explain away the human love of magic. It is only to help myself and my fellow witches to refine our work.

Psychology

To change your mind

It's all in your head. While this theory is sometimes used as an insult rather than an explanation, there is a very large contingent within the broader neopagan, metaphysical, and magical communities who embrace this view as essential. The art of inducing the altered states of consciousness described throughout this book is, to an extent, a psychological exercise.

When this strand of theory is embraced to the exclusion of other theories, you may hear that deities and sundry spirit beings are archetypes and that magic changes the consciousness of the magician, not the world directly. You will hear talk of self-hypnosis and personal growth. This is to say that magic works because we are accessing deeper parts of our minds in order to make meaningful shifts in our perspectives. Sometimes this psychological explanation can become more occult when paired with the widely embraced magical notion that the individual is a mini-version of the universe, and so in a Hermetic sense, a change in individual consciousness and control is echoed in a larger way outside the self. You may hear this idea reflected in language such as, "microcosm/macrocosm," "as above, so below," and "as within, so without."

When drawing on this model, ritual and practice is meant to dig into hidden parts of the self, to cultivate will, self-knowledge, self-control, and imagination for making change within the magician. As one aspect of our own perspective, we see the development of the witch as critically important for expanding and refining their practice. Both your strengths and struggles matter. We see the freedom in embracing the fullness of our power and in the healing integration of the various and disparate parts of ourselves. We see the fulfilling utility in cultivating focus, awareness, visualization, and personal growth. But we do not see this as the whole story.

Energy

To change metaphysical energy

The concept of energy, meaning a universal spiritual force, is widely embraced not just by witches but by a good swath of broader society. It is not uncommon to hear non-witches say that something has *good energy* or *bad vibes*. An energy-based explanation is that magic works because the practitioner correctly identifies and uses spiritual energies inherent to or emanating from things to achieve their ends.

This is not energy as physics defines it, and this model of magic can go awry when its adherents try to force this spiritual theory into the realm of accepted, contemporary science. Typically this is appealing because as a frankly vulnerable minority, we sometimes hope that mixing our magical beliefs with science will lend validity to our spiritual practice. But, the methods of science and the methods of spirituality are distinct and when we muddle them, both spirituality and science can get shortchanged in the process.

There are two ways to think of spiritual energy—the energy of a thing and the energy connecting things, although it is all one. To speak of a thing's energy often comes in familiar contemporary forms such as, "rose quartz is good for love magic" or "rosemary is a solar herb." These are common ways to talk about the ingredients used in natural magic, and even when witches do not directly use the word energy in this context, we are still essentially referring to the spiritual energy of a thing. When speaking of the energy between things, we are trying to describe how one thing (a spell ingredient, for example) can act on another thing (a spell target, for example). The energy between things is about connection and movement and so we use metaphors to reflect that. We might say magic is a spider web connecting all things, and to work a spell is to tug on the corner of the web to shift it a bit in your intended direction. We might say magic is a pond, and a spell is throwing a rock in the pond to create ripples.

As many contemporary witches have been raised within an energy-laden ideology, it is up to each of us as we progress on our paths to discern exactly when and where this energy paradigm works for us. As is expected, each witch will find their own unique answers.

When drawing on this model, ritual and practice is meant to refine the magic worker's awareness of and ability to manipulate spiritual energy. There are usually fairly clear-cut steps in this kind of work. 1) Know or intuit the energetic properties of things. 2) Raise the energy or call it out from the materials. 3) Send the combined energy toward your target. 4) Ground or release the remaining energy into the earth so that your energetic balance is restored. Some of this raised energy may come directly from the witch, but much of it is drawn from tools, ingredients, and other parts of nature in order to be shaped and directed by the witch. Within this model, you are most likely to encounter tables of correspondence in which the spiritual energy of a plant, an astrological sign, or an element are all tied together by a commonality in their innate energy.

When taken as one aspect of our perspective, we do perceive and work with spiritual energy. But we do not see this as the whole story.

Spirit Alliances

To change your relationships with spirits

Spirits are specific autonomous beings—a life force, a spirit-person. We form mutually beneficial relationships with these folks, and they lend us their magical power and do work for us as allies. In some instances this can be coercive—perhaps you have heard of magicians summoning spirits by threat and forcing them to enact the magician's will. That is more of a hostage situation than a proper alliance. As we choose to work, it is always mutual and consensual, a communion and conversation. It is a give and take. We do not *use* allies, whether they are gods, ancestors, trees, birds, fairies, or any other non-human person. We work *with* them.

Some practitioners of magic focus on working very directly with deities or a deity, as it is defined within their theological framework. This is a kind of spirit work. And although the external trappings may look wildly different, it is also a kind of spirit work when a witch honors the plant they are infusing and asks it to lend its spiritual power to the resulting brew.

Because of our embrace of animism, some employment of the spirit/ally theory, in our tradition, is essential. It is, of course, not required to the exclusion of the others. When drawing on this model, ritual and practice is meant to communicate with, exchange offerings with, and work together with (largely) autonomous spirit beings.

Okay, now which model do you choose? Just kidding. You're a practical witch, just do what works. Use your knowledge of the models for refining your workings.

Which Theory? Yes!

Psychology, energy, and cooperation with spirits: Yes. That's probably how the magic gets done. These models are true. And also, at times, untrue. The truth is probably more complicated than any of it, but thinking about our workings through these models helps us to 1) be self-aware, 2) be intentional, and 3) have a tool for thinking critically about our own claims and those of others. Put together, those three benefits can have the effect of making a contemporary witch more knowledgeable, flexible, and powerful.

For much of my generation, our early teachings focused on the energy model, with a dose of the other models. What is sometimes called something's energy is sometimes better described as sensing the spirit of a person, with "person" here in its broadest sense, of course. And we are not so much *raising energy* from passive things as we are entrusted with weaving together the magic of diverse people or entities who work with us. In other words, it is a significant shift of perspective (not just semantics) to say I am *working with* rosemary, this piece of limestone, and my elderly elm rather than to say I am *using* them. It can become an arrogant folly that would limit the power of magical work to not allow the rosemary, limestone, and elm the space to work as whole, enspirited persons. We all work best when our whole selves are genuinely engaged in consensual work. Why draw a bit of energy out of a plant when you can ask the plant to work with you as an honored friend or ally? With their whole self that plant can engage in the task, often teaching the witch as they work together.

That said, there is so much validity and utility in working with themes of spiritual energy, and with engaging intentionally with your own spiritual energy and that of those beings around you. Indeed, for most witches new to the path, the concept of grounding and centering one's own energy is important work. The emphasis of the psychological model on the importance of your own mind and its relationship to the cosmos is also valuable. Clarifying your intention for spellwork, and bringing your daily, external actions into alignment with it is essential. Working to understand the internal blockages and constraints on the free-flow of your power as a witch is deep, significant work.

So use the distinction between models to help you structure your workings and to refine places where you have room to grow as a practitioner. Are you raising non-person spiritual energy and then sending the resulting mixture to make some change? Are you communicating with distinct, sentient *persons* or spirits and relying on them and their innate abilities and autonomous power to make change? Are you trying to shift your own perspective so radically that you make change in yourself that will ripple through the world? The steps in your ritual can reflect whichever models, and combination of models you are using. It can help you prepare properly, do the work mindfully, and assess your level of success. I encourage you to mix and match mindfully to make magic.

The Central Role of Altered States and Will

Whatever combination of theories you deploy to conceptualize a given piece of magical work, the skill of altered-state induction will be required to some extent. This is treated most heavily in the Hedgeriding chapter because the degree of alteration is strongest in that practice. Additionally, the language of *intention* is a popular way to describe what a person wants or what the purpose is behind a certain action. Another way to describe this is as a person's will. The will or intention of magic is not a passing flight of fancy but a deep focus rooted in mind and emotion. All magical theories depend on the fundamental combination of altered states and a clear, firm will.

Reflection

1. Have you (knowingly or unknowingly) been working primarily with only one model? How has that been working?

2. What is your gut reaction to this way of laying out separate ways of understanding magic?

3. Is there a model that you have not worked with at all or have not worked with as much? If so, how could you integrate that model to expand and freshen your work?

4. Choose a magical working that you have performed—elaborate or simple—and dissect which parts of your words, movements, actions, and intention map onto each theory.

Practice

- Create two rituals, spells, or sundry magical workings. Each should draw primarily on a different magical theory.

12

SPELLCRAFT

If you have experienced magic only as Hollywood special effects, then you may be disappointed when you light a candle, speak a spell, and—at least as far as any noticeable results go—nothing happens. But if you've ever experienced magic in your own life, a serendipitous moment when something seemingly impossible happens (a call from a distant loved one the moment you are thinking about them, for example), then you already know that movie magic is just a metaphor for what magic really is: the uncanny, irrational, wonderful, awful power of change. We don't really expect to fall in love and get married in the collapsed timeframe we see in a two-hour romantic comedy, so why do we expect magic to be glowing sparks shot from the tips of wands?

So, how do we think of spellcraft? Spellcraft is one kind of magic. A spell is a ritualistic formula designed to bring about a specific, intentional effect, which is usually meant to take place squarely in this world. Spells usually have a written or spoken component, as well as a physical component of materials, gestures, and ingredients. Spells can range from the very simple to the very complex and draw on or originate from a wide variety of magical currents, cultures, and folkways. Consideration of magical theory can help guide the specifics of spellcraft as well.

Spellcrafting is work. Spellcraft and spellwork are synonymous for the excellent reason that we have to put in some effort to get results. We *do* things, *make* things in order to have an effect. We might think our labor starts when we sit down at our altars to craft a specific talisman bag, but most often our real labor starts when we plant the seed that becomes the basil we later dry and add to that bag.

Sometimes people get caught in a very specific aesthetic trap of fearing that their altar has to look just so, or that they need to buy expensive ritual daggers, imported herbs, or large crystal grids to be able to do the work of witching. However, this is not necessary and sometimes not even desirable, as it can be at odds with the values of being grounded in your own locality and ancestry. Instead, I prefer to make, grow, and forage many of my tools and spell ingredients. It is lovely to work with a small, holed stone from a local river-bed knowing that I am doing my part to keep that river healthy and strong, rather than purchasing a piece of moldavite or opal that might have been mined in harmful circumstances. Although we all have a different sense of what is beautiful, there is no single correct style to witchcraft. *It just has to work, and it often works best when built upon your sense of place, theory of magic, and spiritual ancestry.*

The Grammar of the Grimoire: Magic as a Language

I find myself charmed by the notion of dusty, leather-bound tomes, stuffed with old, powerful words to work as my enchantments. This idea charms many of us, and indeed there are real traditions of using books of magic, or grimoires, for spellcraft. If it interests you, there are many traditional grimoires available. But the word itself—grimoire—gives us a hint to the practical nature of casting spells; *grimoire* shares linguistic roots with grammar. And one way to understand spellcraft is as a language.

It is a language we witches share with the other denizens of this world and the Otherworld, which is why it is so useful to us. Spellcraft is a language of magic that transcends our limited human linguistics. All the bits and bobs—the yarn, candles, herbs, and bones are adjectives and verbs. The gestures, words, and techniques are parts of speech, and we weave them together in meaningful ways just as we weave words into sentences and paragraphs. We can quote old favorites and write new treasures. And as we further develop our craft, our own style becomes clear. As your spellcrafting style develops, take notice and keep notes, and soon enough you may find that you have an informal grammar of your own. The only way to develop it is to dive in, do the work, and see how it turns out.

Witch Crafts: Types of Spellwork

We witches of the Forest's Edge work many kinds of spells, and many spellbooks old and new are available as references. The spells we work rely on our inherent powers and on the strength of our allies. And as with all our magic, each witch's spellcraft is drawn from their relationships with spirits and their rootedness in ancestry. Here is a taste of the variety:

- **Candles and Fire Spells**—We often think of witches sitting by burning candles as they do their spellcraft, but the power of fire can often *be* the work of magic we do. Some of us use candles as a way to honor ancestors, spirits, or saints, and some roll candles in herbs and burn them as spells unto themselves to help with particular needs or outcomes. We also sometimes use fire as a ritual tool, as when we light fires to represent spirits or members of our tradition when we are far away, or even when we use bonfires to burn things as a way of purging their energy from us.

- **Fiber Crafts**—These supposedly mundane domestic tasks traditionally assigned to women (including knitting, sewing, and weaving) are powerful ways of working magic. Knotted charms worked into a prayer shawl make a spell someone can wear, for example. But yarn, string, fabric, dye, and knots can also be used by those with no special skills. Sometimes during a harvest holiday, some of us gather to use an outdoor loom to weave together natural materials and yarn as a way to create a magical representation of harvest and creation, one that remains outside until the next holiday while it slowly releases its magic into the land.

- **Poppets and Dolls**—There are a lot of misconceptions about using dolls in magical work. For example, many people like to call these sorts of dolls *Voodoo dolls*, but that's a misnomer because the African-derived traditions of Voodoo (or more properly, Vodun) don't usually use dolls and definitely not in the way they're depicted in films and television. Many European magical traditions, however, *do* use doll-like figures, called *poppets*, as a way to represent someone in a spell. They may bless that doll using herbally infused waters, place that doll in a freezer as a way to make someone "chill out," or insert pins or mark the doll with symbols to enact things like healing or harming on an individual. (This is where another misconception comes in, as most people only think of using the "doll and pins" method as a curse, when it is just as likely to be a way to target a specific blessing or healing energy for a person.)

- **Potions, Brews, and Teas**—We love green growing things and all manner of creatures in the mushroom family at the Forest's Edge. Many of us work with these allies in spells, and also love making our own incense, soaps, tinctures, magical household cleaning products, and teas out of plants and fungi we've lovingly grown or foraged. You'll find everything from mugwort infusions to help open awareness for hedgecrossing and dreaming to bathing blends used to remove bad luck or add good luck to a person's life.

- **Sigils and Wards**—The process of creating art is a kind of magic all on its own, but the creation of pictorial imagery for magical purposes makes up its own branch of magical work. People within this tradition craft *sigils*, or magical symbols, by drawing particular figures representing natural features, letters or runes, astrological signs, specific spirits or deities, or other things that hold personal significance. These sigils might be carried in a pocket or purse, carved into something wooden, or even incorporated into the room decor of a home as a way of creating an ongoing magical presence in that space. Sometimes these symbols are created with the intention of using them for a while, then destroying them ritually (by burning, for example), and in some cases they can become a long-term ward that protects a particular space.

- **Spoken Charms**—Some spells are simply said aloud or whispered under one's breath as a way of getting results. Anyone who's ever said a quiet little prayer for a parking space and suddenly found one will know what it feels like when a charm like this works. These can be some of the easiest spells to do in terms of the resources required: all they need is breath and intention. However, they also frequently take a lot of effort in terms of focus and mastery and may incorporate certain ritual gestures and hand motions as a way of activating them.

- **Talismans**—This is a big category that can encompass a wide variety of magical works. For example, a small bag stuffed with different herbs that's carried with you can be a type of talisman, but so can a rabbit's foot or a lucky coin. Most often talismans are carried or worn. There are some talismans, however, that also get kept in the home or even your car as a way to offer protection or other blessings.

- **Written Charms**—These are much like the sigils and wards already mentioned, only they depend less on artistic interpretations and symbols and more on the use of specific words or spells written out and carried or placed somewhere they can have an effect. Written charms are usually done on paper but can also be incorporated into artistic charms, talismans, or even chalked on things like clothing, buildings, or walkways to create specific magical effects—even graffiti can be magical!

These are just a few kinds of spellcraft, and most spells don't fit easily into a single category. Spells frequently use more than one of these methods, so a knitted charm may become part of a charm bag filled with herbs and blessed with a magical tincture, for example, combining a variety of magics into one final object.

Spells arise from need and depend on available resources now, as always. Taking time and working with precious materials can lend power to a spell. For example, English cunningfolk sometimes chose more expensive (to buy) or time-consuming and unpleasant (to make) parchment over cheaper, easier paper for important written charms, and we can do similarly in our own ways. But spellcraft must also be practical, so we often make do with what we have. Not everyone has the skill to weave fabric to sew into a charm bag, but they may be able to fold up a piece of paper with some herbs inside, mark it with a sigil, and carry it in their purse as a talisman. That sort of improvisational approach—rooted in tradition but adapting to the individual's situation—is what makes spellcraft so unique and powerful.

Ingredients and Animism

I have a love/hate relationship with using the word *ingredients* in spellcraft. Of course, I like the practical, life-giving connection to the language of cooking. But sometimes that word is used in a way that implies a passive lifelessness to those ingredients. It will come as no surprise that I would rebel heartily against that notion. If you see the rose petals in your spell only as a symbol of love or only as a thing to be used, you are not only slighting the rose itself but also short changing your spellcraft. If you honor and work with the rose as a being with a spirit, then those rose petals can be coworkers or allies, consensually adding their power to yours in your spellcraft. Of course the flipside to this animistic approach to ingredients is that you may pick up a stone that looks perfect for a spell you're planning and feel an intuitive "No!" You'll respect that and replace the stone, searching elsewhere for a willing participant who wants to be in relationship with you. While that may be a bit of extra work, well, spellcraft is work.

Most of the magic done in spellcraft relies on the belief that all things are interconnected or linked together. If you have not already, you will encounter tables of correspondences used in spellcraft that link plants, animals, stones, spirits, colors, and astrological occurrences with specific symbolism or outcomes to help you select appropriate ingredients. Read these tables as a window into how one person (or tradition or publishing company) sees the interconnections between these things. You, as a practicing witch, may experience these relationships differently.

Timing

Sometimes much is made of the timing of spells. If you are strongly drawn to astrology, books on ceremonial magic may give you relevant insights into astrological correspondences and calculations for ritual, such as planetary hours. If those particularities are not a large part of your craft, then consider the possibility that the best time for a spell is when you need it. Much of the time, we do a spell for just that reason—not under a different astrological sign but now! There are also often other practicalities to consider. Maybe the peak of the sun at midday on a Sunday would be an auspicious time, but Sunday night is when you'll have some uninterrupted free time. Each witch must decide for themselves how much timing matters. Like the purchase of materials, it should not be a barrier.

Ultimately, timing a spell is about integrating the spell into the rhythm of the world such that its effects can ripple smoothly outward in harmony with that world. You are part of the world, and your need may simply dictate the correct timing. When there's a bit more flexibility to be found, the familiar rhythms of your life can point to good timing. Time of day, day of the week, season, moon phase, and individual biorhythm are the key variables for timing your spellcraft. When considering timing, don't forgot the possibility of flipping a spell inside out. If you want to do a spell to increase a certain thing, but the moon is waning (traditionally a time for banishing, release, introspection), you could consider flipping the spell around to release barriers to having that certain thing. When feeling unsure about timing, or a spell generally, do not hesitate to deploy your divinatory skills for discernment. As with many things, many witches prefer the liminal edges of timings—such as dusk or the moment when winter shows the first stirrings of spring.

Seasons are fairly intuitive to work with, but so much magic is too time sensitive to wait. But when doing slow-acting, long-term magic, listening to the rhythm of the seasons can add a resonant depth to the work. When considering days of the week, you can work with the etymology of the day's name, traditional associations, or your own associations. Which day feels like a new beginning to you? It may be Sunday because of the calendar, or another day because of your work schedule. Planetary hours is one way of working with time of day, but it's much simpler to consider it a bit like seasons, but faster—a solar cycle in twenty-four hours. Morning, as the sun's strength grows, would then be similar to spring as a time to emphasize newness, fertility, and drawing in positive influences. A similar logic can be extrapolated to any time of day.

Perhaps even more important than these external timings are your own biorhythms. You may love the freshness of working at dawn, but I may feel sluggish, spacey, and resentful at being up so early. Our bodies contain rhythms of their own, particularly with regard to the regulation of hormones, that may or may not reflect outer markers of timing. These rhythms are often associated with menstrual cycles and that is salient, but so too are rhythms of wakefulness and sleepiness, anxiety and relaxation, high energy and low.

For those witches who menstruate, you may find that in terms of spell timing, your bleeding is similar to the new moon or winter. The part of the follicular phase after menstruation would then correspond to spring or the waxing moon, with the time around ovulation being akin to summer and the full moon. The luteal phase after ovulation and before the next period corresponds to fall and the waning moon.

Honoring one's own bodily rhythms, menstrual or otherwise, is a way of appropriately including ourselves in cycles of nature that we consider. Not only is this an acknowledgment of our own place in nature, but it is also eminently practical because if you are in a low-energy, biorhythmic downswing, that likely won't lend itself to an enthusiastic, outward-focused piece of work. In fact, most of us work according to our biorhythms unconsciously, but bringing these patterns into conscious awareness allows us self-empathy, discernment, and choice.

Creative Process and Altered States

Because spells are a kind of ritual, no matter how pragmatic the goal, the material from the Creating Ritual chapter applies here. Like many other rituals, you may find yourself adapting folkloric or otherwise published material to your own purposes. Perhaps you've found a spoken charm that you love and are designing a physical component to go with it. Or maybe you've found a spell that relies on herbs that don't grow in your region. It is not only okay—but also desirable—to adapt. The more adaptation you do, the more easily the grammar will come to you. You will create quite a bit of your own grammar over time, perhaps recorded in your own grimoire or maybe learned by heart.

While I have spoken against mistaking an expensive witchy aesthetic for doing magic, it is nonetheless true that witches—like all humans—have aesthetic preferences. While aesthetics do not create the magic, shaping your spellcraft to your aesthetic preferences can be a signal to your own consciousness to begin the shift to magical awareness. Aesthetics speak to what appeals to the senses, and ritual is meant to do just that. While it should never be a barrier, considering what looks, feels, and smells like magical power to you can help you decide how to adapt or create spells.

As with all magical ritual, there is an important element of altered state creation in spellcraft. While hedgeriding entails powerfully altered states, the altered state of spellcraft is subtle and less frequently discussed. In spellcraft your awareness expands to encompass, with a sense of immediacy, the interconnectedness of everything. The language that best describes this expanded awareness is that you are seeking *empowered interconnectedness*. Within that interconnectedness, you feel yourself present and active, able to push and pull to shape reality. We've already talked about envisioning that interconnectedness as a tremendous spider's web with you as the spider. That is to say, you can sense movement in the web as a spider does. You can reweave the connections and create change.

Most of the time this state is light enough that you can slip into it with the rhythms and sensory signals of preparing for and beginning the ritual of the spell. If you are finding this expanded awareness difficult to achieve, practice is excellent training. Another option is to include more rhythm and repetition to the spells (long chants, movement, percussion). If the idea of practicing without trying to create a specific piece of work has appeal, then try practicing with visualization. Set the mood with simple things you might do at the beginning of spellwork (for example, sit at your altar, light a candle, light herbal incense, make offerings) and then focus your imagination on the image of being a spider in the web of ties between all things (or substitute another image of empowered connectedness that works for you). Work on this until you aren't just seeing the image but can *feel* the reality of it.

Reflection

1. Why do spells fail sometimes? Is there anything a spell couldn't achieve?

2. How would you define *magic,* using your own words? How would you define it if you were trying to explain it to someone else?

3. What is your current relationship with spellcraft? Where are you comfortable? Where can you identify growing edges?

4. Is there a particular current or cultural tradition of magic that holds a special appeal for you (medieval grimoire, powwow, Hoodoo, for example)? Why does this current call to you?

5. Are there spells you absolutely would never do? Why or why not?

Practice

- If you have not already, locate a source of traditional spells within your own ancestry. Many of us have more than one line

of ancestry to explore. Depending on the culture you're working with, this may be difficult or easy. You may be reaching
back to pre-modern material, to the biased words of colonizers,
to the condescension of old-fashioned anthropologists, or to
folk magic within a religious context other than your own. You
do not need to adopt these practices wholesale, but select one
to adapt to your current needs and experiment with giving it
a try.

- Experiment with movement in spellcraft as ability allows.
  While the stereotype is of a barely moving witch seated before a
  candlelit altar, experiment with walking, dancing, large gestures, jumping over or physically crossing something.

- Experiment with unbridled intuition. In direct contrast to
  the appeal to history and folklore above, try using no written
  resources and no advance preparation of materials. Ignore the
  rules and trust your inner knowing.

- Don't have a pretty spellbook or grimoire. Is that shocking?
  If it's working well for you to keep a beautiful book of magic,
  then by all means keep on. If you have a pretty book, lying life-
  less and ignored because the pressure to make entries beautiful
  and perfect is suffocating, then tuck it away and get an ugly,
  ruled, school notebook. Let it be messy. It's just notes on your
  work.

13

MAGICAL ETHICS

Do you occupy a unique space between clear and sweeping ethical restrictions and mindlessly following whims? Same here. Most witches do. This is another way that we occupy the liminal spaces betwixt and between. Extensive lists of rules or broad dictums have a powerful appeal. In those moments of emotional complexity and uncertainty, there is something soothing in grabbing hold of the clarity of simple, received wisdom, shared universally among a community. But I cannot offer you the reassuring certainty of enforced rules for all moral choices.

Instead, I am part of a community of diverse people who support each other in defining and upholding our own individual moral codes within our shared worldview, along with a few specific rules to keep the community itself well functioning. If you are not part of a tradition, coven or other supportive community, it can be very helpful to reach out to at least a few fellow witches (in person or online) with whom you can share mutual support and guidance.

Witches at the Forest's Edge strive to live ethical lives. Our ethics arise out of being witches on a green path. All of nature can be both glorious and terrible, comforting and vicious. We witches walk a crooked path in a dynamic balance of light and dark. We value integrity between belief, speech, and action. We honor learning and growth. There is no magical practice that is forbidden.

For witches, mature ethics are about sovereignty, or self-rule. We seek the power to know and the power to choose for oneself. Most folks go through life operating from a defacto sense of right and wrong, but for witches, seeing clearly (our inner workings and outer circumstances) is the first step to intentional, empowered choice.

The Costs of Practicing Magic

As witches we accept and embrace our power. We are wildly, deliriously free to use it as we choose with no oversight committee guiding our actions. Ultimately, we have our own minds and hearts, and the wisdom of chosen others, to determine whether a spell, a divination, or a ritual is aligned with who we want to be and with the kinds of relationships we want to honor. It is a considerable responsibility especially since magical practitioners would rarely be held accountable in the broader community. After all, if I punch my neighbor in the nose, she's not confused about what happened and could press charges. If I work magic on her, for good or ill, it is impossible to empirically connect me to the results or pursue remedy through the justice system.

Although few can call our power to account, that doesn't mean our magic is without cost to ourselves or to unintended others. Just as spirituality is not solely focused on the development of oneself, so too magic depends on working with and within the community of plants, animals, ecosystems, spirits, and deities. When we marshal our resources to do magic, we work within the truth that we are not isolated islands, but rather we are selves-in-community. This truth yields both power and consequence, and at the Forest's Edge our sense of magical ethics arises from our appreciation of interconnectedness and reciprocity.

Traditional witchcraft does not forbid any spellcraft or other magical practices. We cultivate the skill to both hex and heal as needed, as all of existence contains this sort of ebb and flow. While nothing is forbidden, neither should the practitioner be careless or unaware that actions have consequences. Before doing malefic (harmful) spellcraft, examine your motives, your emotions, and your logic. Ask your deities, ancestors, and other spirit allies for guidance. Use divination and consider mundane solutions as well. Then, if the time comes for harmful magic, consider magnitude. You would not use a firebomb to resolve a spat with a grumpy neighbor, so it would be unreasonable to use the magical equivalent. When performing magic of any kind, be prepared to accept the consequences. There is a cost to be paid for the work you do.

Plucking the spider's web creates a ripple of vibrations through the web to which you are not immune. Exactly how to resolve this cost can vary. We're all too familiar with the phrase "you reap what you sow" and this is sometimes true, but a witch doing malefic magic is trying to avoid exactly that. The specifics of how you curse can lend themselves to figuring out a means to avoid any unpleasant aftereffects. A solid starting point is to make a significant offering that restores the overall balance—almost a literal payment. In fact, it can be a literal payment if you like to give money offerings to good causes. Typically, there should also be an element of spiritual self-cleansing in any form, from herbal baths to sweeping. If the curse was performed indoors, consider also a spiritual cleansing of the location.

Nature is red in tooth and claw, and as part of nature, so are we witches. It is our right to fight hard with magic, and with that right comes responsibility. Believe in your magic enough to treat it like your mundane actions. It's up to you whether you want to use the magical equivalent of killing someone or not, but if you do, be prepared to pay the cost. You can redirect the flow of water in a creek, but not without some work. The first piece of that work is finding your own moral center and deriving a practical code of ethics from it.

An Ethical Structure

This section offers one way to think deeply about magical ethics without dragging you through the history of ethical thought or moral philosophy. There's nothing at all wrong with that, but, you know, sometimes there are spells to cast. So, here's a down and dirty map to digging through the layers of a witch's ethics so that each of us can see clearly:

practices $\rightarrow$ ethical code $\rightarrow$ values $\rightarrow$ moral center $\rightarrow$ sources

With each arrow we dig a little deeper to find what lies beneath. Being ever so fond of the darkness, it is my inclination to start from the bottom and work our way up.

Sources

Buried in the deepest, darkest earth of our minds and hearts are the sources of our ethics. The reality is that our sources are almost always a hodgepodge and often only semiconscious. Some sources are easy to name and others we only really uncover after taking a hard, self-searching look. Often a crisis or conflict of some sort compels us to dig into these ethical origins. Some common sources are childhood experiences or patterns, significant conversations with loved ones, family beliefs passed down and repeated, painful life experiences, the cultural and religious elements of family or mainstream culture, and stories and books. Any source can be right, effective, powerful, mature, or mindful. But as working witches, we can find ourselves confused and struggling, particularly when we are not consciously *aware* of our sources. Our most ethically empowered state is when we know our sources and consciously affirm them and their relevance to our present practice.

Values

The emerging themes from these sources are values. These are the concepts that you hold in very high regard. Some prevalent examples are loyalty, fairness, care for nature, independence, humility, and compassion. The tricky bit is that mostly we are all so busy paying our bills and dealing with our families or heath crises or whatever goes on in our lives that we all make choices based on our values *but* without having time to closely examine what underlies those values. So again, the radical freedom of witchcraft gives us a powerful reason to look at our values and give voice to them. Because, in truth, we all live our values. We all live our values in our magical lives as well. The question for us as ever-evolving witches is: Can we consciously and confidently name and affirm those values that shape our lives?

Values are formed and informed by the environment we live in and what elements of that environment we perceive that we can control. They are formed and informed by our basic primal need to survive and feel safe, but also by our human needs to connect with others, to understand or find meaning in our experiences, to experience physical, emotional, and mental comfort, and to express ourselves. And it is a very common experience to hold a value intellectually but not live that value practically. Reasons for this could range from simple lack of awareness to extreme fear for one's life.

Moral Center

A moral center is *a constant dynamic conversation* with our values. When external situations arise and bump up against our values, that interplay between inner commitment and outer action is the moral center. We can discover what it is we truly value by examining the way we live our daily lives, how we interact with others, how we handle money, what makes us happy, unhappy, and angry. We can ask ourselves the "why" questions, check our actions against our values, and adjust as needed.

As witches, being aware of and truly honest with ourselves about our moral centers is important work. In order to work both in this world and in the Otherworld, we must know and trust ourselves; and to intentionally shape reality through magic, we must be able to intentionally shape ourselves.

Ethical Code

Your ethical code—your rules for self-rule—are your own. Since on the whole traditional witches do not have an ethical dictum or list of thou shalt nots, this code can be unique to you, unless you are also bound by a specific community's rules. While piecing together your values and their underlying sources is a challenge, it is also the work that helps you be intentional about choosing your own principles to guide your actions.

Practices

Holding all of the knowledge and clear sight from the deeper layers discussed above, ultimately you decide what is best. Like all of the above components, this is typically done with only partial awareness, but full awareness breeds freedom. So, while each individual process is unique, a healthy, thorough, and functional application of ethical decision-making typically involves the following components:

- **Listening:** We listen to our inner truths and we listen with care to the perspectives of others. Listening to spirits, gods, and sundry allies is also key for a witch.

- **Questioning:** Adopt a stance of curiosity and ask questions of the situation and oneself. Questions range from objective facts to motivations and intentions. Questions can be quantitative and qualitative, objective and subjective. Reflective questioning is a strength that refines understanding.

- **Weighing:** Which of your values is the most relevant in this situation? What are the benefits and drawbacks? What are the consequences, and how will you and others pay the price?

- **Choosing and Accepting:** We select a course of action and deal with whatever consequences, beneficial or detrimental, result from the action.

This last part of the process is often how those who live strictly by their own ethical system, rather than by an externally imposed moral code, can be identified. Conscientious objectors and all those who break laws or otherwise transgress codes that the larger group lives by in order to pursue a course of action they think is right are valuing their own moral code above the moral code of their community. By doing so openly and honestly, they accept the consequences of their actions. History, fiction, and myth provide us with many examples of this, both laudable and infamous.

Reflection

1. List the top five things in life you value. Base this list on what you see when you look at the way you live your life, not on what you think you should list. Be honest with yourself without judging. If you find yourself holding a value that you feel you would not want others to know you value, ask yourself why you are ashamed and whether you might be willing to change that value.

2. What do you think a witch's values should be? In answering this question, consider what role a witch plays in their community, how that witch conceives of the spirits, and how they interact with the ecosystem. List the top five values of this envisioned witch. How do the values of that witch you envision match up with your values? Do you see any changes you want to make? Why?

3. How well do you listen to yourself when you are faced with a decision? How well do you listen to others? What voices do you value most when deciding something important in your life? Your own? Your family members'? Authority figures'? Experts in a given field?

4. What laws in your society would you be willing to break and why? Under what circumstances? What rules, taboos, morals, or laws would you be willing to break if you knew you couldn't get caught? Translate this idea into the practice of magic. Can you list things you might be willing to do magically that you would not do practically? Examine why this might be problematic or defend why it would not be.

5. Based on the values of your moral center, what questions might you ask yourself when faced with a dilemma or decision?

6. What kind of listener are you? Is it easy for you to consider another's point of view, or difficult?

7. What kind of questions might you ask someone with whom you have a disagreement? What would you want someone to ask you if they did not understand your point of view?

8. How prepared are you to accept the consequences of your actions? What sort of consequences would prevent you from taking a course of action, even if you felt it was the right course? In what situations would you proceed with a course of action, no matter what the consequences were?

The Witch at the Forest's Edge

As I reach the end of writing this book, it is the autumnal equinox, a perfect time for the satisfying harvest of finishing a project. I gathered wild persimmons from the forest with my family yesterday, so today my daughter and I will make shortbread and persimmon puree for a harvest picnic. Those thick-barked persimmon trees have been alive longer than I have, and this fall's fruit has been a year in the making. This book has been growing slowly over time too, ready for harvest in the fall. If not for the years of teaching and writing and magic with inspiring witches, it wouldn't be what it is. I hope the harvest is bountiful for you wherever you are on your path. The ways that I talk of witchcraft here are not suited to everyone and do not define the gloriously broad group of people who identify as witches. I celebrate the diversity, but my, how cumbersome it would be to be forever writing "witches . . . " and adding "who practice like this, but not all witches do, and that's okay." I guess if you've gotten this far, the way you're called to practice is probably similar enough.

We are, each of us, the witch at the forest's edge. We are always at the edge of something, one foot here and one foot there. We step over and back, over and back, ever riding the hedge. Our spirits are beckoning us deeper, deeper into the forest dark, where the moss remembers your feet, where someone in the branches is watching. You belong here, if you want it. The enchanted life is good one, brimming with connection and magic. And a hard one, full of work and responsibility. There are so few limits for the traditional witch, so few rules. So while ideas can be offered, each of us must get our nails dirty and scratch out our own way—if we're lucky we get to do that with a community of fellow scratchers. I am lucky like that, and I enjoy sharing that good fortune.

The contents of this book are a beginning and the basis of how I and my tradition practice traditional witchery. But if this is the trunk, the branches are infinite. Each subject from hedgeriding to local ecology to folk magic is only a start. Your research into and practice of whatever tickles your fancy can be nearly endless and fascinating and particular to you. If you know other witches, it can be fun to share your interests and be the one who knows about something who can help others with that subject. The notions of spiritual ancestry and being a green and local witch are woven throughout this book because they hold a special place. Intertwined with one another, digging deeply into your peoples, your histories, and your lands, makes your witchcraft unique. It gives your practice deep roots and strengthens a network of meaningful connections.

You can spend a lifetime learning and refining your practice if you choose. And, you can just take time to settle into your rhythm and appreciate it. Don't fear the cycles of practice. The time and energy that you devote to your craft will wax and wane and shapeshift through the seasons of your life. It doesn't make you less of a witch. You are just living with cycles, like the rest of nature. The magic is yours, a witch unto yourself. You are beholden to no one but connected to many as you stand at the forest's edge.

May the strong ones guard you
May the old ones guide you
May enchantment surround you
This day and all the days of your life.

Resources

This resource list is organized to correspond with each chapter. The material in each chapter is intended as a framework for further explorations into your roots and your interests. I hope these resources are helpful as you continue to explore. In the interests of space and sanity, I have included only a few individual podcast episodes in the resource list, but the podcast I co-host, *Betwixt and Between* on Apple Podcasts, addresses many of these subjects such as ancestors, faeries, divination, hedgeriding, local geology, and more. There are many more magical podcasts that can offer free resources and fun conversation such as *New World Witchery, Inciting a Riot, Rune Soup, Borealis Meditation,* and *Down at the Crossroads.*

Worldview and Spirituality

- *Ecopsychology,* Theodore Roszak, Mary E. Gomes, and Allen D. Kanner

- *Ecotherapy,* Linda Buzzell and Craig Chalquist

- *I and Thou*, Martin Buber

- *Re-Enchantment of Everyday Life, The*, Thomas Moore

- *Spell of the Sensuous, The*, David Abram

Communing with Spirits

- *Cunningfolk and Familiar Spirits*, Emma Wilby

- *Encyclopedia of Spirits, The*, Judika Illes

- *Fairies in Tradition and Literature, The*, Katherine Briggs

- *Fairy-Faith in Celtic Countries, The*, W. Y. Evans-Wentz

- *Grimoire for Modern Cunningfolk, A*, by Peter Paddon (especially the ancestor section)

- *History of Irish Fairies, A*, Carolyn White

- *Irish Fairy and Folk Tales*, by W. B. Yeats

- *Secret Commonwealth, The*, Robert Kirk

- *Serpent Songs*, ed. Nicholaj de Mattos Frisvold (bits and pieces in sundry essays)

Also check out folklore and religious history of all sorts—especially that derived from the region of your (blood or spiritual) ancestors and that of the place where you live. There are also various Internet resources. As a starting point:

- *Betwixt and Between* podcast, "Ancestors," episode 15

- *https://newworldwitchery.com,* "Fairies in the New World"

- *www.patheos.com,* "Top Ten Questions about Ancestor Veneration"

- *http://wildhunt.org,* "Ancestral Practice Altars and the Mighty Dead"

Spiritual Ancestry

These are derived from my sense of spiritual ancestry, and may or may not apply to yours. Please consider them a starting point and inspiration.

- *Between the Living and the Dead,* Éva Pócs

- *Cunningfolk and Familiar Spirits,* Emma Wilby

- *Ecstasies,* Carlo Ginzburg

- *Folkloric American Witchcraft and the Multicultural Experience,* Via Hedera

- *Mind in the Cave, The,* David Lewis-Williams

- *Orlean Puckett*, Karen Cecil Smith

- *Popular Magic*, Owen Davies

- *Prospero's America*, Walter W. Woodward

- *Seven Daughters of Eve, The*, Bryan Sykes

- *Treasury of New England Folklore, A*, B. A. Botkin

- *Visions of Isobel Gowdie, The*, Emma Wilby

Cultivating Spirit Senses

- *Real Witches' Craft, The*, Kate West

Hedgeriding

- *Betwixt and Between* podcast "Hedging Your Bets, part 1" and "Hedging Your Bets, part 2," episodes 47 and 48

- *Cunningfolk and Familiar Spirits*, Emma Wilby

- *Images and Symbols*, Mircea Eliade (trans. Philip Mairet), chapter 1, "Symbolism of the 'Centre'"

- *Magical and Ritual Use of Herbs, The*, Richard Alan Miller

- *Shamanism*, Mircea Eliade

- *Shamanism,* Graham Harvey

- *Shamanism,* 2nd edition, Michael J. Winkelman

- *Shamans,* Ronald Hutton

- *Singing with Blackbirds,* Stuart Harris-Logan

- *To Fly by Night,* Veronika Cummer, ed. (I consider this required reading)

- *Visions of Isobel Gowdie, The,* Emma Wilby

Divination

- *21 Ways to Read a Tarot Card,* Mary K. Greer

- *54 Devils,* Cory Thomas Hutcheson

- *Bones, Shells, and Curios,* Michele Jackson

- *Holistic Tarot,* Benebell Wen

- *I Ching,* revised edition, Thomas Cleary

- *Ogam,* Erynn Rowan Laurie

- *Planets for Pagans,* Renna Shesso

- *Taking Up the Runes,* Diana L. Paxson

Theology

Just a few that I have enjoyed.

- *Ancient Goddesses,* eds. Lucy Goodison and Christine Morris

- *Becoming Divine,* M. David Litwa

- *Mabinogion, The,* trans. Lady Charlotte Guest

- *Oxford Dictionary of Celtic Mythology,* James MacKillop

- *Queen's Festivals, The,* Mother Mary St. Peter

- *Rebirth of the Goddesss,* Carol P. Christ

- *She Who Changes,* Carol P. Christ

- *Wisdom Has Built Her House,* Silvia Schroer

A Green and Local Craft

Please note that some of these books are specific to my region. They are given as examples because each region will have its own books and other resources.

On Animism:

- *Animism,* Graham Harvey

- *Demons and Spirits of the Land,* Claude Lecouteux

- *Encyclopedia of Psychoactive Plants, The,* Christian Rätsch

- *Gaia's Garden,* Toby Hemenway

- *Geology Lab for Kids,* Garrett Romaine

- *Honeysuckle Sipping,* Jeanne R. Chesanow, illus. Norma Cuneo

- *Pharmako Dynamis,* Dale Pendell

- *Pharmako Gnosis,* Dale Pendell

- *Pharmako Poeia,* Dale Pendell and Gary Snyder

- *Readings in Indigenous Religions,* ed. Graham Harvey, specifically "Ojibwa Ontology, Behavior, and World View," A. Irving Hallowell; and "Animism Revisited: Personhood, Environment, and Relational Epistemology," Nurit Bird-David

- *Spell of the Sensuous, The,* David Abram

- *Tradition of Household Spirits, The,* Claude Lecouteux

Also:

- EPA Ecoregions data: *www.epa.gov,* "Ecoregions"

- USGS Ecoregion maps, descriptions and trends: *http://landcovertrends.usgs.gov/*

- *www.worldwildlife.org,* "Terrestrial Ecoregions"

The Practical Use of Magical Theory

- *High Magic*, Frater U.:D.:

- *High Magic II*, Frater U.:D.:

- *Magical Writings of Thomas Vaughan (Eugenius Philatethes), The*, Thomas Vaughan

Spellcraft

- *365 Days of Hoodoo*, Stephanie Rose Bird

- *Black Pullet, The*, Anonymous

- *Cunning Man's Handbook, The*, Jim Baker

- *Earth Power*, Scott Cunningham

- *Encyclopedia of 5,000 Spells*, Judika Illes

- *Grimoires: A History of Magic Books*, Owen Davies

- *Making Magic*, Brianna Saussy

- *New World Witchery*, Cory Thomas Hutcheson

- *Popular Magic*, Owen Davies

- *Spellcrafting*, Arin Murphy-Hiscock

- *Long-Lost Friend, The,* John George Hohman (ed. Daniel Harms)

About the Author

Christine Grace is a longtime teacher of the Craft and a founder of the Forest's Edge Tradition of witchcraft. She is cohost of the *Betwixt & Between* podcast, covering a variety of topics in witchcraft and everyday magic. She has graduate degrees in theology and mental health counseling from Vanderbilt University. Connect with her at *www.christinegracebetwixt.com* or @awitchbetwixt on Instagram.

To Our Readers

Weiser Books, an imprint of Red Wheel/Weiser, publishes books across the entire spectrum of occult, esoteric, speculative, and New Age subjects. Our mission is to publish quality books that will make a difference in people's lives without advocating any one particular path or field of study. We value the integrity, originality, and depth of knowledge of our authors.

Our readers are our most important resource, and we appreciate your input, suggestions, and ideas about what you would like to see published.

Visit our website at *www.redwheelweiser.com,* where you can learn about our upcoming books and free downloads, and also find links to sign up for our newsletter and exclusive offers.

You can also contact us at *info@rwwbooks.com* or at

Red Wheel/Weiser, LLC

65 Parker Street, Suite 7

Newburyport, MA 01950